Praise for *The Artisan Herbalist*

A wonderful, insightful introduction to herbalism, *The Artisan Herbalist* provides well-organized instructions on making herbal preparations as well as practical information on how to use plants for health and healing. Beautiful photography highlights and aids in identification of these commonly available plants. Only plants that the author himself has used and knows well are included so one is presented with first-hand knowledge and expertise. A surprising and welcome addition to the book is a chapter on starting your own herbal business, which provides enough detail to get you headed in the right direction. Altogether, a thoroughly delightful, practical, and well-organized introduction to the uses of plants as medicine and food.

ROSEMARY GLADSTAR herbalist and author, *Rosemary Gladstar's Medicinal Herbs*

We seem to be wandering into a new way of living, and self-sufficiency has become much more important. Learning to make medicine from easy to find herbs is a huge step in the right direction. *The Artisan Herbalist* leads the new herbal enthusiast to learn and embrace the plants and how they can help us. Seasoned herbalists will find many pearls of wisdom within these pages that can broaden their own knowledge.

TINA SAMS editor, *The Essential Herbal Magazine*, author, *Herbal Medicine for Emotional Healing*

In *The Artisan Herbalist*, Bevin offers his personal experience and formulations, guiding the reader to easily create their own infusions, teas, tinctures, oils, salves, and balms—his instructions are simple, clear, and informative in Bevin's conversational style.

SUSAN BELSINGER educator, herbalist, author,
The Culinary Herbal: Growing and Preserving 97 Flavorful Herbs

Bevin Cohen has created a masterpiece! Not only is this book beautiful, but it is highly useful. From the basics of making remedies, including a great selection of herbal monographs and recipes, to key tips and details for getting an herbal business up and running, including legal requirements, labeling, marketing, and pricing, this is the book every beginner herbalist should have on hand to start on their herbal path.

KRISTINE BROWN RH (AHG), author, *Herbal Roots zine, Herbalism at Home, The Homesteader's Guide to Growing Herbs,* and *Nature Anatomy Activities for Kids*

The Artisan Herbalist

MAKING TEAS, TINCTURES,
AND OILS [AT HOME]

BEVIN COHEN

new society
PUBLISHERS

Cover design by Diane McIntosh.
Main image: ©Shutterstock Small dropper vial: ©iStock
All interior images © Heather Cohen (unless otherwise noted)
Printed in Canada. First printing April 2021.

Inquiries regarding requests to reprint all or part of *The Artisan Herbalist*
should be addressed to New Society Publishers at the address below. To order
directly from the publishers, please call toll-free (North America) 1-800-567-
6772, or order online at www.newsociety.com

Any other inquiries can be directed by mail to:
New Society Publishers
P.O. Box 189, Gabriola Island, BC V0R 1X0, Canada
(250) 247-9737

LIBRARY AND ARCHIVES CANADA CATALOGUING IN PUBLICATION

Title: The artisan herbalist : making teas, tinctures, and oils (at home) / Bevin Cohen.
Names: Cohen, Bevin, 1979- author.

Identifiers: Canadiana (print) 20200379844 | Canadiana (ebook)
20200379852 | ISBN 9780865719583 (softcover) |
ISBN 9781550927511 (PDF) | ISBN 9781771423472 (EPUB)

Subjects: LCSH: Herbs—Therapeutic use. | LCSH: Herbals.

Classification: LCC RM666.H33 C65 2021 | DDC 615.3/21—dc23

Funded by the   Financé par le
Government   gouvernement
of Canada   du Canada

New Society Publishers' mission is to publish books that contribute in funda-
mental ways to building an ecologically sustainable and just society, and to do
so with the least possible impact on the environment, in a manner that models
this vision.

Y OU'D LIKE TO be self-sufficient, but the space you have available is tighter than your budget. If this sounds familiar, the Homegrown City Life Series was created just for you! Our authors bring country living to the city with big ideas for small spaces. Topics include cheesemaking, fermenting, gardening, composting and more—everything you need to create your own homegrown city life!

- **THE FOOD LOVER'S GARDEN:** *Growing, Cooking and Eating Well* by Jenni Blackmore

- **WORMS AT WORK:** *Harnessing the Awesome power of Worms with Vermiculture and Vermicomposting* by Crystal Stevens

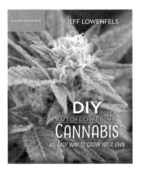

- **PURE CHARCUTERIE:** *The Craft and Poetry of Curing Meats at Home* by Meredith Leigh

- **DIY KOMBUCHA** by Andrea Potter

- **DIY AUTOFLOWERING CANNABIS** by Jeff Lowenfells

- **DIY MUSHROOM CULTIVATION** by Willoughby Arevalo

- **THE ELDERBERRY BOOK** by John Moody

- **DIY SOURDOUGH** by John and Jessica Moody

- **YOUR INDOOR HERB GARDEN** by DJ Herda

#Homegrowncitylife

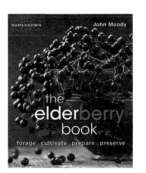

CONTENTS

INTRODUCTION

ELCOME TO THE world of the Artisan Herbalist! Mother Nature's abundant gifts are beneath our every footstep, from the neighborhood park to the deep forest, and throughout this book we will explore the endless possibilities that she so generously offers. Regardless of where you may live, city or countryside, the benefits of herbalism are everywhere and accessible to all.

It would be impossible to include the hundreds of useful plants available to the herbalist. The herbs covered in this volume were selected because they met a certain, simple set of criteria. First, each of the chosen plants is common enough to be foraged or grown in any geographic location. This ensures that anyone interested in exploring the beneficial flora of their region will gain insight from this book. Secondly, and most importantly, I have personally worked with every herb included in these pages. Developing a relationship with the plants that provide us with our food and medicine is paramount to the health and wellness of any practitioner, and I would be remiss in my responsibility to the reader if I included herbs with which I am not intimately familiar. The language throughout this book is intentionally offered in the style of formal academia, following the precedent set before me by the likes of Pliny the Elder, Pedanius Dioscorides, John Gerard, and Nicholas Culpeper, all whose works I reference within these pages.

The study of herbs and their uses is a lifelong endeavor, and experienced herbalists can use this book to deepen their knowledge, while those just first exploring the realm of herbal medicine will find the information to be an indispensable introduction and influence on their research. A majority of *The Artisan Herbalist* is focused on the practical application of herbal knowledge, offering tangible and useful formulas to assemble and produce a wide range of wellness products for personal or commercial purposes. Within the entries discussing the individual herbs and their uses, I've included historical references and etymological derivations as well as cultural phenomena relating to the plants, when applicable. Just as the herbalist must learn the botanical identity of each plant in the *apothecary*, or herbal medicine cabinet, the cultural identity of our herbs is just as valuable. These two identities are inseparable to those who truly wish to understand the qualities and benefits of the herbal allies with which we work.

While the practice of herbalism is certainly enjoyable, the practitioner must understand and accept the gravity and responsibility that comes with it—from harvesting and processing herbs to manufacturing and administering medicines. When gathering herbs from the wild, it's vitally important to avoid harvesting from areas exposed to environmental pollution, such as roadsides or waste sites. Additionally, the herbalist will wish to avoid areas that have been sprayed or treated with synthetic herbicides or pesticides. Only healthy, clean herbs should be chosen for use in medicine making. The responsible forager also understands the significance of sustainable harvesting practices. Only gather what is needed and never more than one-third of a plant's local population. When harvesting from a tree or large shrub, never take more than one-sixth of the plant's foliage or branches. Overharvesting an herb is irresponsible and unsustainable. We must remember to think not only of ourselves, but of future generations as well.

Great care must also be taken with the formulation and distribution of herbal wellness products. When developing recipes, it's expected that the herbalist will choose the highest-quality ingredients whenever possible, whether the items being crafted are for personal or commercial use. In addition to this, the herbalist must remain committed to continuously developing their relationship with the plants that they work with, while simultaneously expanding their knowledge to guarantee the safety of their family, friends, and potential customers. We are never the master, always the student.

With this book in your hand, a bit of curiosity, and an interest in the herbal world, you are well on your way to making teas, tinctures, and oils at home. Let these pages inform and inspire as you continue your journey down the path of the Artisan Herbalist.

MAKING TEAS, TINCTURES, AND OILS AT HOME

HERBAL
TEAS

*W*HEN CONTEMPLATING THE use of herbs in daily life, surely one of the first methods that will come to mind is the brewing of delicious herbal tea. Whether it's a mellow peppermint tea to soothe the stomach or a more invigorating rosemary and cinnamon blend to heighten the senses, herbal teas have become synonymous with wellness, self-care, and the many benefits of home-based herbalism. While the traditional beverage of "tea" is made by steeping the leaves of the Asian evergreen shrub *Camellia sinensis,* in these pages we will be discussing the herbal counterpart to this drink, crafted from various plants chosen for their flavor profiles and health benefits—plants that can be grown or harvested by any herbal enthusiast regardless of where they live or the amount of available space that can be dedicated to cultivating their own herbs.

With every pot of herbal tea brewed and every cup poured, the artisan herbalist comes closer to understanding the truest essence of the plant from which they imbibe. It is through this sacred ceremony of tea that the herb and herbalist become one.

Gathering Your Equipment

Getting started in the world of herbal teas requires minimal equipment. First, the herbalist will need a kettle and a source of heat for boiling water, whether that's the stovetop in their kitchen, the wood stove of a cabin, a campfire in the woods, or even a barbecue grill at a neighborhood park. If the intention is to brew only a solitary cup, the herbalist will need just a teacup or mug, but if the plan is to brew multiple cups at a time, they will also need a ceramic teapot for steeping their beverage. If a teapot isn't handy, the resourceful tea maker can use a mason jar or any similar container to brew their herbal beverages.

There are a number of options on the market for reusable tea infusers that the herbalist can choose from based on their preferences and needs. The most common of these is likely the tea ball, a wire mesh sphere that holds the herbs during the steeping process; some of these hang from the lip of the tea mug via a hook and small stainless steel chain, and some have a handle that can be squeezed like a pincer to open the tea ball, which is hinged. These types of infusing tools are inexpensive and easy to clean, but after many uses the thin stainless steel parts can bend and will no longer be as effective at keeping plant matter out of the tea.

Another option is reusable tea bags, which are usually made from cotton, muslin, or silk. While these may prove to be a bit more difficult to clean between uses, with proper care they can be used multiple times. Many of these reusable bags will hold a significantly larger amount of herbs than their tea ball-style counterparts, which the herbalist will find quite useful when making larger infusions. When infusing herbs or spices that have been powdered, reusable tea bags are the best choice because they will prevent the plant material from escaping into the brew.

A third choice is a basket-style infuser, which is essentially a fine mesh filter, normally made from stainless steel, that settles into the top of the cup or teapot as the water is poured over the herbs. This can be limiting because the infuser is only effective when the vessel is full enough for the water level to reach the basket and its contents. This style of infuser is also a bit more bulky and difficult to store in comparison with reusable bags, but there are models available that fold up for ease of storage and portability.

Regardless of the type of reusable infuser you choose, once you have one in hand, you are ready to begin creating your own herbal tea blends.

Single-Herb Tea

Oftentimes, a single herb is all that is needed for a successful and enjoyable tea. This is particularly true for the new herbalist; working with each herb as an individual ingredient will help the student fully explore the flavor profile and aroma of the herb as well as its effect on the body and mind.

As the herbalist moves through their studies of the various herbs in their apothecary, perhaps one of the most powerful opportunities to enhance their education is joining their herbal ally in the ceremony of tea. From selecting the herb, to filling the infuser, boiling the water, and then pouring it into the cup, the act of brewing tea can be seen as a moving meditation. Keep your herbal journal handy so you can take notes of what you experience as you spend time with each plant. How does the herb smell as you fill the tea bag or when you inhale the steam from your cup of brewing infusion? Make note of how the aroma makes you feel and what thoughts it may bring to your mind. Upon taking the first sips of the tea, again make notes in your journal of the flavor and the impression the tea makes in your mind. Are you feeling more relaxed? Is the tea warming and spicy, or crisp and refreshing? Whatever your impressions may be, taking the time to document these experiences in your journal is an excellent way to build your herbal knowledge base and develop a deeper relationship with the plants you will be working with.

Creating Tea Blends

Before sitting down to sip and savor a delicious herbal tea, the herbalist must first decide which herbs they will be preparing for their infusion. This decision will certainly be influenced by the intended purpose of the tea; while there are no specific rules to dictate the process, it's a common practice for blends to follow a formula that

▲ Studying a single herb, such as sage, is both productive and enjoyable.

includes a central herb that is complemented by additional ingredients chosen for flavor, balance, and benefit.

This is a perfect opportunity for the herbalist to use the information in their journal. Not only will their single-herb studies come in handy for creating blends, but the herb journal can also be used to make notes and record recipes.

Choosing the central herb of your tea is the first step to creating your blend. Depending upon the purpose of your tea, be it for flavor and enjoyment or for a medicinal brew, this herb will constitute the main bulk of the recipe and should be chosen accordingly.

The additional ingredients will then be selected for their ability to support this main ingredient. Herbs can be chosen for their flavor, to complement the tea's profile or to mask the taste of the first ingredient. If it is a medicinal tea, other herbs can be added to the blend that accentuate the benefits or attributes of the original herbal base.

Additional ingredients can be added at this point to bring balance to the tea. Most commonly, herbs with citrus or floral notes are used in this manner, although any herb that supports the overall flavor of the tea is acceptable.

Steeping and Pouring

Once the artisan herbalist has gathered their equipment and selected the ingredients for their infusion, they are ready to participate in the ancient ceremony of steeping their herbal tea. This is as simple as bringing the water to a boil and then pouring it over the herbs to steep in a cup, teapot, or other heatproof container. It is not wise to use soft plastics for brewing herbal teas.

Typically, when brewing tea with dried herbs, the amount of plant material used is approximately one tablespoon per cup of tea. If the herbalist is using fresh herbs for their tea, they should plan to use three to four times as much plant material.

The length of time that the herbs are allowed to brew depends upon the intended purpose of the herbal infusion. For a simple and delicious beverage, the tea can steep for as little as three to five minutes. For a more medicinal drink, the tea can be left to brew much longer, giving the water more time to extract the chemical constituents from the plant matter. For a significantly more potent beverage, the herbalist can even infuse their herbs in a mason jar that is covered and placed in the refrigerator to brew overnight.

Infusion or Decoction

Many herbal tea blends are crafted from leaves, stems, flowers, and buds, and sometimes from small, thinly coated seeds. With these parts of the plant, the chemical constituents can easily be extracted using the infusion methods just described. Other parts, such as bark, roots, thickly coated seeds, and woody stems, may be more difficult to break down due to their thicker cell walls; in order to properly extract the flavor and medicinal benefits from these parts, the herbalist will use a process known as *decoction*.

Simply put, decoction is the process of boiling the plant material in order to break down the cell walls, which encourages the release of the plant's chemical constituents in a form we can use. This is a longer, slower process than a simple water infusion and can take anywhere from ten minutes to an hour—or even multiple hours—depending on the particular plant in the decoction.

Enjoying Your Herbal Tea

Now that you've brewed the perfect cup of herbal tea—whether for its medicinal benefits or as a simple and delicious beverage—it's time to sit back, sip, savor, and enjoy. Consider complementing your brew with a squeeze of lemon juice, a splash of cream, or a spoonful of local, raw honey while you partake in the time-honored tradition of herbal tea.

TINCTURES

*P*ERHAPS NOTHING ELSE stirs the imagination quite like wooden shelves covered with dusty glass jars of various herbs and old bottles filled with mysterious herbal medicines. Many times, these dropper-capped, brown medicine bottles contain a powerful plant extract known to the artisan herbalist as a *tincture*.

What Are Tinctures?

Tinctures are extracts, similar to herbal teas, but they are created by steeping plant matter in alcohol as opposed to hot water. There are many benefits to crafting herbal medicine in tincture form. Tinctures are quite potent, so only small dosages are typically needed; thus, tinctures can be packaged in small bottles, which makes them more portable and convenient. Alcohol also acts as a preservative, so the herbalist's tinctures will have an extended shelf life, especially when packaged in dark glass and stored in a location away from direct sunlight.

Additionally, tinctures are made using a cool-temperature infusion method, unlike teas, which are brewed using hot water. Many of a plant's most delicate constituents can be damaged or lost to evaporation when exposed to heat. For this reason, tinctures tend to retain more of the potent medicinal compounds found within the plant material. Tinctures are also absorbed into the bloodstream faster than herbal teas, allowing the user to experience results sooner and, quite often, more intensely.

Preparing Herbal Tinctures

When the herbalist is ready to craft their first tincture, the list of equipment they need to gather is actually quite short. Although tinctures are considered to be very potent herbal medicines, making them is a very simple task. Of course, the first thing needed will be the herb or herbs that the medicine maker plans to use. While there are many tinctures available that are crafted with multi-herb blends, it is always wise for the novice herbalist to begin their studies with single-herb formulas. Making medicines with individual herbs will allow the practitioner to properly experience the truest essence of their chosen ingredient. As one becomes more familiar with the herbs in their apothecary and develops deeper relationships with their medicinal plants, creating herbal blends for tinctures will be a more valuable practice. But first, they must take the time to truly understand the benefits and potential risks of each individual herb.

The use of single-herb tinctures is a particularly beneficial practice for the herbalist that has just begun their studies. Making notes of extraction time, coloration, aroma, and flavor—as well as the medicinal effects of each tincture—is a vital step in building the knowledge and experience needed to craft safe and useful medicine.

Along with the chosen herb, the herbalist will also need a container for infusing their tincture as well as alcohol for extraction. For a container, any glass jar with a lid will do, the most popular choice being a canning jar. For the alcohol, there are a number of choices available depending on the herbalist's particular need or preference.

In many traditional herbals, the alcohol chosen for the recipes is brandy, which is usually made from distilling wine. Brandy is a dark and strongly flavored liquor. In modern herbals, the typical alcohol called for is usually vodka or even a higher-proof grain alcohol. Many herbalists prefer vodka because the liquid is clear and the flavor of the liquor is very light. This allows the color, smell, and flavor of the herbal extract to come through in the tincture, heightening the experience for both the medicine maker and the consumer. Vodka is also typically a less-expensive alcohol, which can be an influential factor for the herbalist on a budget.

Regardless of the type of alcohol that is used as the solvent, or *menstruum,* what's important when making a tincture is the percentage of alcohol in the liquid. In the United States, this is referred to as *proof.* Proof is defined as twice the alcohol content by volume in a liquid. For example, a vodka that is 50% alcohol would be considered 100-proof. In Canada and most other places in the world, alcohol content is labeled by ABV (alcohol by volume).

For making quality tinctures, the herbalist should strive to use a menstruum that is at least 80-proof (40% ABV). This strength will suffice for a majority of the herbal tinctures that the artisan herbalist will choose to craft, yet it is still dilute enough to sufficiently extract the water-soluble constituents of the plant material. If the herbalist is working with fresh, high-moisture herbs such as berries or roots, they may want to consider using a more potent solvent of around 70% ABV. This can be accomplished by mixing a blend of half 80-proof vodka and half 190-proof grain alcohol. For tincturing gums and resins, the herbalist can use pure 190-proof grain alcohol.

Crafting the Tincture

Once the herbs and alcohol have been selected, the herbalist is ready to begin crafting their tincture. There are two distinct methods of tincture preparation, both of which have a place in modern herbalism. The first style of tincture-making is often referred to as the *folk method.* This is simply packing the herbs into the glass jar until it is about half full (for dry herbs) or three-quarters full (for fresh herbs) and then adding the alcohol until the jar is full and the plant material is completely submerged.

The second method is a more precise technique, generally known as the *standard method.* With this style of tincture formulation, the herbs and menstruum are measured in a ratio of weight to volume.

▲ When your herbs have steeped in alcohol for a sufficient amount of time, your tincture is then ready to be strained and bottled.

For example, if the tincture being crafted calls for a 1:2 ratio, the herbalist would use 1 part herb to every 2 parts menstruum. While herbalists tend to rely on metric measurements for their formulas, as opposed to dry and liquid ounces, these numbers refer specifically to proportion regardless of the measurement system being used. These formulas, including the strength of alcohol being used, should be recorded in the medicine maker's herbal journal so the tincture can be reproduced again with similar potency. This is especially important if the herbalist plans to offer their tinctures commercially. The standard method of tincture production is also necessary if the herbalist is working with herbs that are potentially toxic when consumed in high doses, but it is highly recommended that the herbalist begin their studies working with herbs that are generally regarded as safe.

Regardless of the method of measurement chosen, it's important that the herbs are completely covered by the liquid—avoiding exposure to the air—to ensure they will not mold during the extraction process. Once covered, a dowel, skewer, or similar item should be used to quickly poke down through the submerged herbs to release any air bubbles that might be present. Then simply cap the container, label it, and place it away into a cool, dark place to steep. You will need to remember to shake the jar every few days. The label should include the name of the herb or herbs being extracted, the alcohol used as the solvent, and the date of production. Any cupboard or closet will do for storage, as long as it remains cool and dark for the duration of the process. The mixture should be allowed to extract for six to eight weeks. Don't forget to shake your jars!

Bottling Your Tinctures

After your tincture has steeped for the recommended time, it will need to be strained and then bottled. Straining the tincture can be done with simply a cheese cloth and a funnel. Once you capture the herbs in the cheesecloth, be sure to squeeze out as much of the absorbed liquid as possible, either wringing by hand or pressing with a spatula or similar tool. A large funnel with a built in screen can also be purchased through brewing supply companies, and this type of equipment will prove to be quite useful for this chore. Another option is to use a French press for squeezing every precious drop of tincture from the extracted plant material, so it is not wasted. The artisan herbalist can also consider buying a tincture press, a specialized piece of equipment for this task. The leftover herb, once thoroughly pressed, can be composted or discarded.

The completed tincture can now be bottled into any size container, but the typical packaging is one- or two-ounce, dark-colored glass bottles with included dropper tops, for ease of use. These small bottles are portable, and the brown or blue glass helps protect the herbal medicine from sunlight. Green glass bottles are also available, but, although they are more protective than clear glass, they are not as effective as the brown or blue glass options.

Alternative Solvents

Although a traditional tincture is made with an alcohol solvent, alternatives are available for herbalists interested in crafting medicine that is alcohol-free. The technique for creating non-alcoholic extractions is the same as described above, but a different menstruum is used. Typically, these types of medicines are made using glycerin or, occasionally, vinegar to extract the chemical compounds from the plant material. By definition, tinctures are extracts made with an alcohol solvent, and the alternative, alcohol-free products are referred to as simply *extracts*. Glycerin extracts are typically chosen for treating children because of taste, as well as the safety concerns related to alcohol consumption by minors. It is important to note that this style of product is not as potent and will not have as long a shelf life as its alcohol-based counterpart.

Using Herbal Tinctures

One of the many benefits of including tinctures in the herbal apothecary is their potency. Since they are quite strong, the recommended dosages are significantly smaller than something taken as a medicinal tea. While the specifics vary depending on the herb being used or the desired outcome, the dosage for a tincture is generally a half dozen drops to a teaspoon per serving. This can be taken straight, under the tongue, or even diluted in water, tea, or another beverage. It is generally accepted that the sublingual application of a tincture will be more direct and fast-acting than a diluted dose, but both techniques are certainly effective.

INFUSED
OILS

ERHAPS THE MOST versatile item in the artisan herbalist's arsenal is the herb-infused oil. The diversity of potential applications, as well as the multitude of products into which infused oil can be crafted, truly makes this form of extraction a powerful ally in any apothecary. The medicine maker may choose to use their oils to create salves, balms, and lotions or, in a pure oil application, either topically or for culinary use. Whichever method they decide upon, they will find great satisfaction in the ease with which these products can be made and how beneficial and powerful the resulting medicines are.

Gathering the Ingredients

Infusing herbal oils is a simple yet remarkably satisfying process. As with the preparation of any other extraction, the first step is choosing the proper ingredients and gathering the needed equipment. Aside from the herbs and oils, a vessel is the only other mandatory tool, and for this job, a glass jar is highly recommended, particularly one with a screw-on lid. Glass is far superior to plastic or metal, especially for long-term storage of your medicinal oils. Clear glass is suitable for this task, as the oil will be stored in a cool, dark location throughout the extraction process.

Choosing the Right Oil

When crafting herbal oils, the focus of most recipes is typically on the herbs to be used, their medicinal benefits, and the desired purpose of the final products. While these are all obvious and important considerations, many herbalists fall short by not taking more time to understand and properly select the other main ingredient: the oil.

Just as the herbalist selects particular herbs based on their active chemical constituents, the oils used (also derived from plants) each have their own characteristics and chemical constituents. This suggests that different oils have different uses, benefits, and applications. Taking the time to choose the proper oil—one that complements and enhances the herbs being used in the formula—will increase the product's potency as well as the herbalist's success.

The oils most commonly used by at-home herbalists are olive, coconut, grapeseed, and sunflower. These are all are fine choices; which to use will depend on what you are trying to accomplish and your personal preferences. If carbon footprint is a concern, consider purchasing oils that aren't imported from far away. Sometimes it's possible to source oils that have been pressed locally. You can even try pressing your own! Small, home-scale oil presses are available for purchase and may be a viable option for herbalists interested in a more do-it-yourself approach to their craft.

When searching for quality oil to purchase, be sure to look for oils that are labeled as cold pressed or expeller pressed. You do not want oils that are produced using heat (which degrades the nutritional value of the oil), or those that are extracted by the use of chemicals. Chemically extracted oils are *refined* oils; they have very little flavor, scent, or color but also lack any significant nutritional value. While they may serve a purpose for some, these are not the high-quality oils that should be chosen for an herbalist's work. Chemically extracted and purified oils should be avoided, especially when the herbalist is crafting topical, oil-based wellness products.

Infusing Your Herbs

Once the appropriate herb(s), oil, and vessel have been selected, it's time to begin the extraction process. Simply pack your chosen herbs into the vessel, then add the oil, pouring until the plant matter is completely submerged and the level of the oil is above the herbs by approximately one to two inches (three to five centimeters). Next, using a small tool such as a dowel, skewer, or even a pencil, poke through the submerged plant material a few times to release any air that may have been trapped. Once there are no more bubbles floating to the top, place the lid on the container, and label the vessel.

Labeling and Storage

Thorough labeling of any herbal extraction is an important step toward an organized and functional apothecary. For infused oil, the artisan herbalist will want to include the list of herbs (and their quantities) used in the formula as well as the oil chosen as the solvent. Including the date that the infusion was prepared, as well as when the extraction will be complete, is also necessary. This information can also be logged into the medicine maker's herbal notebook for future reference.

Once labeled, the herbal oil should be placed in a cool, dark place to steep. Generally, four to six weeks is an appropriate amount of time for this process. If the medicine maker has used fresh herbs in the extract, then six weeks is as long as the herbs should be left in the oil. But if the herbalist has used dried herbs, the concoction can sit longer—or until it is needed. This difference in recommended extraction time is due to the water content of the fresh herbs and the possibility of the plant material molding or the oil turning rancid. After the herbs have been strained from the oil, this is no longer a concern.

Once the oil extraction has steeped for the recommended period of time, the herbalist needs to filter the plant material from the infused oil using cheesecloth, or something similar. A wire mesh strainer will suffice for this chore, as will a funnel with a built-in screen (these can be purchased at brewing supply stores or online). Whichever tool you use, be sure to thoroughly filter the oil, leaving no plant material behind.

Once the infused oil is strained, it is ready to be used, either through direct application or as the main component in a lotion, balm, or salve. The oil will likely have absorbed many of the characteristics of the herbs, often expressing their beautiful colors, smells, and flavors. Take a moment to appreciate this delight for the senses and the medicine that these herbs have so generously offered to share.

Using Heat to Expedite Extraction

Occasionally, herbalists may find themselves in need of a certain component for their herbal formula that they don't already have prepared in their apothecary. Sometimes the luxury of waiting four to six weeks for an oil extract just isn't possible. When this situation arises, the artisan herbalist turns to heat in order to shorten the extraction period and produce useful medicinal oils in a fraction of the time. Heat extraction, although much faster, does not always produce oils of equal value. Simply put, these oils may not be as potent as the ones produced through the traditional slow-extraction method, but the technique can still be useful when time is of the essence.

There are a few methods of heat-based extraction that the medicine maker can choose from, depending on the equipment they have available. The most common method involves the use of a Crock-Pot or slow cooker. The herbs can either be placed directly into the pot with the oil, or the herbs and oil can be put into a jar and then placed into the Crock-Pot with a few inches of water. With either technique, the cooker is then placed on low heat to gently warm the herbs (with the cover on, if possible). The herbs can be left this way for anywhere from 6 to 24 hours to steep. The longer the concoction is allowed to brew, the more potent the infused oil. It is crucial that the heat remains low; too much heat will degrade the nutritional and medicinal values of the herbs and the oil and ruin your extraction.

If a Crock-Pot is not available, the herbalist can imitate this technique using a double boiler. Again, avoid overheating the oil; use a slow, low heat to ensure a quality finished product.

▲ Carefully pour the hot oil and wax mixture into containers.

Using the Infused Oils

There are many times that herb-infused oils can be used "straight up," that is, without any further processing. They can be utilized for a variety of culinary applications or prescribed for topical, medicinal uses such as massage oils and scalp tonics or applications for burns, bug bites, and abrasions. In other situations, herb-infused oils are used to craft various wellness products such as salves, lotions, and balms. Essentially, these products are crafted by blending the oils with beeswax or other stiffening agents, creating what are, in essence, herbal oils made portable. These products are easy to take on the road, stored away in the traveling apothecary; in many instances, they are much easier and less messy to apply than pure oils may be. There are certainly a few differences from one product type to the next, but the most definitive factor is the ratio of oil to wax in the formula. The greater the wax content, the more firm the final product.

Crafting a Salve

The herbal salve is possibly the most well-known wellness product crafted from infused oil, and it can be used for a wide range of ailments and conditions. While the formula can and should be adjusted by the artisan herbalist to their preference, the basic ratio is 1.25 parts beeswax by weight to 16 parts oil by volume.

BASIC SALVE RECIPE

1.25 oz. (28.35 grams)
beeswax (weight)
16 oz. oil (473 ml) (volume)
This yields approximately
18 oz. (volume) of final
product.

SAGE ADVICE To test the
consistency of your salve or
balm before pouring, a small
amount of the blended oil can
be put on a plate and placed
in the freezer to cool, similar
to how one would test a jam
or jelly.

1. The medicine maker will use a double boiler to melt the beeswax into the oil while gently stirring the mixture to blend. If a double boiler is not available, the herbalist can substitute with a stainless steel bowl placed over a pot of boiling water. Remember, this bowl will become very hot, and caution must be used to avoid any injury.

2. Once the wax is melted and blended into the oil, carefully pour the hot oil mixture into containers. Any size or shape container will do, depending on need and desire, but soft plastic should be strictly avoided. Remember, this oil will be quite hot, so thin plastic is not a safe choice.

3. As the oil and wax mixture cools, it will solidify and the final consistency of the product can be tested. Be sure to label the container of herbal medicine for easy identification in the future. You have now created a freshly handcrafted herbal salve!

Crafting a Balm

While the terms *balm* and *salve* are often used interchangeably, there is one distinct factor that differentiates the two product types: the ratio of wax to oil. Balms are stiffer and firmer because they have more beeswax in the formula than their salve counterparts. Generally, the ratio is 1 part beeswax by weight to 4 parts oil by volume.

BASIC BALM RECIPE

The process for blending the oil and wax is the same as with a salve. Often, the final container is a plastic lip balm tube, but any style of container can be used to hold the product. Remember to properly label your containers to avoid confusion.

Crafting a Lotion

For a variety of skin issues, herb-infused lotions are fantastic products. They are simple and soothing to apply, and it is easy to cover a large area of the body with just a small amount of lotion. This is due to the fact that the quantity of beeswax in a basic lotion formula is significantly less than what is recommended in an herbal salve or balm. This higher oil content creates a softer, more spreadable product that is quickly absorbed into the skin after application.

There are a variety of formulas that herbalists can use when crafting their handmade herbal lotions, only some of which include water as an ingredient. Products that contain no water are often referred to as *body butters,* while the term *lotion* is reserved for formulas that do include water. Depending on the herbalist's preference, there are some pros and cons to consider when choosing whether or not to use water in a recipe. It's recommended, when possible, to trial both styles of product in order to determine what works best for the individual herbalist. It's only through experimentation that the medicine maker will find the techniques that speak to them and their practice.

Possibly the greatest drawback to incorporating water into a lotion blend is the drastically reduced shelf life of the final product. For herbalists who choose to use water, they must decide to either accept this fact and plan to refrigerate the final product to extend its shelf life somewhat, or they will need to add a preservative to the lotion to ensure its stability. If the herbalist is planning to offer the product commercially, this decision is even more important. While being sure to disinfect tools and using distilled water will aid in increasing shelf life to some extent, the growth of mold in the lotion is nearly inevitable without the use of a preservative. There are a few options available: rosemary essential oil and vitamin E oil are effective during short-term storage, and synthetic preservatives are a viable long-term option.

Crafters deciding to use water also have the additional opportunity to infuse this water with herbs, adding another layer to their blend, thus increasing its effectiveness, or in some cases even changing its appearance and/or odor.

BASIC LOTION RECIPE

1. In a double boiler, combine beeswax and oils. Slowly melt the beeswax and gently stir until fully mixed. Remove the mixture from heat and allow it to cool until it begins to solidify. Add water and stabilizer, if desired, and then blend. An immersion blender is a very useful tool for this job. Once the mixture is fully blended, pour into containers.

    The basic lotion recipe calls for the use of beeswax, which serves as an emulsifier (stabilizer). Since oil and water do not mix, they would eventually separate out if the beeswax were not included.

1.5 oz. beeswax (weight)

5 oz. coconut oil (volume)

9 oz. oil (volume)

8 oz. water (volume)

Optional: stabilize with vitamin E oil (one tablespoon), rosemary essential oil (10–30 drops), etc.

BASIC BODY BUTTER RECIPE

The process for blending the oil and wax is the same as with a lotion. Since the body butter does not contain water, it is thicker and firmer than a lotion; it is also considerably more shelf-stable.

In addition to the soft and creamy lotions and body butters that the herbalist can create, there is also the option of crafting a lotion *bar*. With its higher ratio of wax to oil, this product is more like a salve or balm than a lotion, but it is a portable option that the herbalist may find useful. The recipe is very simple and can easily be customized to fit a variety of needs.

1.5 oz. beeswax (weight)

6 oz. coconut oil (volume)

3 oz. shea butter (volume)

BASIC LOTION BAR RECIPE

2.5 oz. beeswax (weight)

3.5 oz. oil (volume)

3 oz. shea butter or coconut
oil (volume)

The process for crafting the lotion bar is similar to the previous recipes, but once the ingredients have been properly melted and blended, the mixture can be poured into silicone molds to cool. Silicone trays or muffin tins can also be used. If the artisan herbalist does not have access to silicone molds, regular baking containers can be used if they are first sprayed with a non-stick spray for ease of removing the bars after cooling.

It's important for the artisan to remember that these basic recipes are simply starting points for learning the process of crafting various herbal products. The formulas are meant to be tweaked and adjusted to fit the medicine maker's needs and preferences as they develop their craft. It is through experience that the herbalist will decide on which ingredients they prefer to create with and which form of product works well for them.

Alternatives to Beeswax

Some herbalists may decide—for themselves, for family, or for their clients—not to use beeswax in their formulations. This can be due to a vegan lifestyle or for various other reasons. Although beeswax is mentioned a number of times in the previous recipes, there are certainly alternatives to this ingredient.

The most popular alternative to beeswax is carnauba wax, a vegetable wax obtained from the leaves of the Brazilian palm tree, *Copernica cerifera*. Carnauba is the hardest natural wax available and is used widely in various commercial cosmetic and pharmaceutical applications.

Emulsifying waxes are another alternative. These products are made from either vegetable or petroleum-based waxes that are treated with detergents to create a white, waxy solid; these types of waxes are used quite extensively in commercial lotions, balms, and other blends.

While it is certainly up to the individual to choose which ingredients they prefer to use in their products, it's important to remember that everything applied to the skin is absorbed directly into the body; it is wise for the artisan herbalist to always choose the most-responsibly harvested, ethical, and safe ingredients for use in their formulas.

OUR
HERBAL
ALLIES

HERBS
OF THE
PARK,
FIELD,
AND
FOREST

BOTANICAL WONDERS AWAIT the artisan herbalist at every local park, nearby field or wooded forest. Nature's endless bounty and healing medicines are everywhere and available to all that are willing to seek them out.

CHICKWEED

Stellaria media

Common chickweed is an easy-to-identify spring herb that can be found growing in lawns, meadows, parks, and most open spaces. Although native to Eurasia, this plant has naturalized and can be found around the world. A low-growing herb, often forming mats, chickweed can be identified by the single line of fine hair growing up one side of its stem and the five deeply lobed petals of its flowers. In fact, the flowers are so deeply lobed that at first glance, they can appear to have ten petals. *Stellaria media* means "amongst the stars," in recognition of the herb's flower, which resembles a star.

Chickweed was widely utilized by traditional herbalists across Europe; in the 1600s Nicholas Culpeper suggested its use for a wide variety of skin conditions including redness, itching, and rashes. The astringent qualities of *S. media* would lead the artisan herbalist to use this plant for similar ailments. Chickweed is cooling and will also relieve the irritation caused by insect bites, eczema, and psoriasis. The herb is best prepared in an oil infusion or tincture for these applications. Tincture of chickweed is known to be a highly effective medicine for drawing out a splinter from the skin.

This delicate herb is a popular and nutritious spring green and is renowned for its ability to strengthen the liver and soothe the digestive system. Topical treatments using the fresh herb as a poultice or a salve can be useful as a cooling treatment for varicose veins and hemorrhoids.

Chickweed is also valuable in helping the body release retained water and ease bloating, and it has even been suggested that it encourages weight loss. When utilized for its diuretic nature, the herb is often combined with dandelion (*Taraxacum* spp.) in teas or salads. There are a handful of old herbals that recommend chickweed juice or water as a weight-loss supplement, and, although the herb is a diuretic and a mild laxative, it is likely chickweed's mild effect as an appetite suppressant that would be most beneficial in this regard.

◄ The distinct flowers of spring-harvested chickweed are delicate and beautiful. AVOFERTEN: SHUTTERSTOCK.COM

DANDELION

Taraxacum spp.

The beautiful yellow flowers of this common herb are a welcome sight to herbalists in the summer, although many people still mistakenly consider this useful plant to be a noxious weed. There are many species within the genus *Taraxacum*, all of which are considered dandelions, and, although there are species native to North America, the two most common, *T. officinale* and *T. erythrospermum*, were both introduced from Europe. Dandelions are edible from blossom to root and can be found in meadows, parks, lawns, and just about any open, sunny location.

The bitter herb dandelion has been used medicinally for millennia, with some of the first recorded uses being from ancient Egypt. It's thought that the genus gets its name from a combination of the Greek words *taraxos,* which means "disorder," and *akos,* for "remedy." The specific epithet *officinale* refers to the plant's long history of use in the apothecary. Many of the traditional uses for this herb are still employed today, including treatments for the liver, gallbladder, and digestive system. The bitter leaves are used as a stimulant for the system, typically ingested as a tea.

Dandelion roots are considered to be the most medicinally potent part of the herb. As the herb prepares itself for dormancy, it stores its energy in the root system, so it's recommended to use roots that are dug in the fall, whenever possible.

Dandelion roots have been prescribed as a diuretic, a mild laxative, and for general organ health, although the kidneys and liver seem to benefit the most from the use of this herb. The roots should be brewed as a decoction or tinctured for the most effective medicine. Tincture of the leaves and blossoms of dandelion is also beneficial.

Topically, dandelion has been used for its antibacterial properties and is thought to be quite useful for acne, especially in tincture form. When infused in oil and crafted into a salve or lotion, the herb often is helpful with rashes, insect bites, and other skin irritations as well as offering relief from eczema and psoriasis.

◀ The roots, flowers and deeply lobed leaves of dandelion are all useful to the Artisan Herbalist.

ELDER

Sambucus nigra

Elder is a plant steeped in history and mythology. Although species of elder can be found in most places in the world, this fast-growing shrub has long been held in high regard in Europe, with most of its traditional uses tracing back to that continent. Outside of the apothecary, elder has been used as a hedgerow tree, and its branches have been made into flutes, whistles, and even pop guns due to the ease with which the soft center pith can be removed. Perhaps the most well-known use for the fruits of this tree is the brewing of elderberry wine, but this sacred herbal ally is also a valuable medicinal plant.

It is critical that the artisan herbalist be aware that aside from the flowers and ripe, cooked berries of this plant, every other part is considered poisonous and unfit for human consumption. This includes the bark, stems, leaves, and seeds. The most popular elderberry products are cooked and strained, such as wine, jellies, and syrup, and this processing makes them safe to enjoy. Elderflowers, on the other hand, can safely be used for teas and tinctures and even battered and fried as fritters for a unique summer treat.

The two most widespread species of *Sambucus* in North America were once considered separate species (*Sambucus canadensis* and *Sambucus cerulea*) but are now commonly thought to be subspecies of *S. nigra*. They are recognizable by their scraggly appearance, bluish-black berries, and their tendency to grow in moist soils and open areas.

Syrups and tinctures crafted from elderflowers and berries have long been prescribed for their antiviral properties. They are recommended for boosting the immune system and are widely utilized against the influenza virus. Traditionally, this herb was also suggested for bronchial and pulmonary complaints, and elder is still used for these purposes today.

The flowers and leaves of elder have been prepared in an oil extraction for the topical relief of muscular pain and bruises and to stimulate tired muscles. A strong brew of elderflower tea is useful for its astringent qualities and has long been prized for this application.

The flowers and berries of elder can be enjoyed when first harvested or dried to be used in a later season.

GOLDENROD

Solidago spp.

The showy, golden flower heads of this familiar herb can be spotted on roadsides and in fields and meadows from the late summer into the autumn months. There are about 100 species within the genus, but they are all referred to as goldenrod. While there are differences amongst the species, they have widely been used interchangeably throughout history, although *S. canadensis* and *S. virgaurea* are the two most recorded in herbal literature. Useful as a food source for people and insects, this herbaceous perennial is a valued addition to the artisan herbalist's apothecary.

The name *Solidago* is said to be derived from the Latin *solido,* which means "to strengthen or make whole," and even the common name *goldenrod* attests to the herb's perceived value. The herb has been used by Indigenous North Americans for food and medicine for hundreds of years. The young leaves are treated as vegetables, and the seeds can be utilized as a grain.

Goldenrod is considered astringent and antiseptic. It has been used as a tea for kidney stones as well as for bladder and urinary tract infections. The astringent qualities of this herb can also be useful for tightening and toning the skin and as an aid in the treatment of acne when an infusion is used as a wash.

Although many people believe that goldenrod is the cause of their hay fever complaints, the actual culprit is more likely to be ragweed, *Ambrosia* spp. In fact, tea brewed from the aerial parts of *Solidago* is often beneficial for relieving the symptoms of seasonal allergies. This brew can be especially effective when blended with broadleaf plantain (*Plantago major*). The artisan herbalist can employ goldenrod tincture for similar benefits. This tincture is also useful for respiratory complaints, such as congestion stemming from allergies, flu, or the common cold.

The leaves and flowers of goldenrod can also be infused in oil and utilized in topical treatments for muscular pain, arthritis, and tendinitis. Depending on the situation, the herbalist can choose to simply use the infused oil or to craft the oil into a balm or lotion for ease of application.

Women who are pregnant or breastfeeding should not consume goldenrod

HAWTHORN

Crataegus spp.

The thorny shrubs and trees known as hawthorn are of the family *Rosaceae,* which also includes roses, blackberries, and peaches. With species native across the Northern Hemisphere, these helpful herbal allies can be found growing in a wide variety of environments, and their highly adaptive nature is part of the reason these trees have been widely used for landscaping in yards, streetscapes, and parks. Hawthorn can be identified by their small apple-like fruits that ripen to red in the fall and the thorns protruding from their branches—although there are a few thornless cultivars that have been developed in recent years.

All species of hawthorn are beneficial to the artisan herbalist, although the three most commonly referred to in the literature are *Crataegus monogyna, C. oxyacantha,* and *C. laevigata.* While the fruit of the tree is most widely utilized in the apothecary, the flowers and leaves are also useful. They are considered astringent and anti-inflammatory and can be infused in oil for use on skin conditions such as eczema and psoriasis. Tinctured, the leaves and flowers of hawthorn are recommended for topical treatment of acne or for internal use for digestive issues or intestinal infections. Tea brewed from the leaves has shown to ease a sore throat.

Hawthorn fruits have historically been prescribed for matters of the heart. Traditional herbalism has long maintained that *Crataegus* is beneficial for cardiovascular health, including issues with blood pressure, chest pain, and has an overall positive impact on the heart. It is even mentioned in numerous folktales that these fruits are good for improving the mood and easing the anxiety of those that embrace its medicine.

Herbal tea blends that include hawthorn berries are the most widely recorded method of utilizing this herb, but many modern herbals recommend a tincture crafted from the fruits. In addition to toning the circulatory system and strengthening the heart, this tincture is used to boost the immune system and increase energy and alertness.

◀ The harvested fruits, or *haws,* of hawthorn can be dried and preserved for use all year.

JEWELWEED

Impatiens capensis

The beautiful flowers of this colorful herb are a common sight along ditches and creeks throughout the summer. Native to North America, this species of *Impatiens* is also found growing alongside the yellow-flowered *I. pallida,* and these plants can be used interchangeably by the herbalist. Jewelweed is sometimes called "touch-me-not" thanks to the plant's ballistic technique of dispersing its seeds.

While not typically foraged as a wild-harvested food, due to its bland flavor and tendency to cause digestive complaints when consumed in large quantities, jewelweed has been appreciated for its medicinal qualities for hundreds of years.

In stories told by Indigenous populations, jewelweed is mentioned for its use as a topical treatment for poison ivy. This use for the herb is still employed today. The artisan herbalist knows to directly apply the sap that excretes from the succulent stems of *Impatiens capensis* to the affected area, or to craft a salve or balm using oils infused with the flowers, leaves, and stems of the plant.

An herbalist who plans ahead can gather the aerial portions of this plant, brew them in a potent infusion, and then freeze the resulting tea for future use. Using an ice cube tray or something similar will allow the artisan herbalist to freeze individual "doses" that will bring relief from itching, rashes, insect bites, bees stings, and other surface inflammations. Crafting salves, balms, or lotions from jewelweed-infused oils will provide an even more portable medicine. The effectiveness of these formulas can be increased with the inclusion of chickweed (*Stellaria media*) or broadleaf plantain (*Plantago major*).

Jewelweed can also be tinctured and used as a topical medication for similar applications. Many modern herbals suggest the use of isopropyl alcohol for these extractions, but it is very important to remember that this type of tincture, commonly referred to by herbalists as a *liniment*, is not safe to ingest; it is strictly for topical use only. This jewelweed liniment can be stored in a small spray bottle and applied to the skin as a preventative against poison ivy (*Toxicodendron radicans*) exposure or as a remedy to be used after exposure.

◀ The vibrant color of jewelweed flowers can easily be spotted in open fields and along roadsides.

MOTHERWORT

Leonurus cardiaca

Motherwort is a member of the mint family, *Lamiaceae*, with the typical square-shaped stem, opposite leaves, and pink to lilac-colored flowers. Native to southeast Europe and Central Asia, motherwort can be found growing along roadsides, in fields, and other places where the soil has been disturbed. Due to its high value as a medicinal plant, this herb has been widely distributed and is now naturalized worldwide.

In 1597, the herbalist Gerard wrote of motherwort's use to aid ailments of the heart. He also claimed that an alcohol extraction of the herb could be employed as a diuretic.

Numerous herbalists have followed Gerard's thinking when writing about the herb's value for the heart and cardiovascular system. The herb's specific epithet, *cardiaca,* lends credence to this claim.

Once motherwort was brought to North America, it was quickly adopted by Indigenous populations who used an infusion of the leaves to stimulate digestion, relax the nerves, and as an herbal tonic for menstruating women. *Wort* is an Old English word meaning "plant" or "herb," and as the common name *motherwort* would suggest, this plant has long been prescribed for issues relating to feminine health.

While many traditional herbals recommend the use of motherwort in a tea or potent infusion, modern literature often suggests tincture of *L. cardiaca* as a heart tonic as well as for women's health issues. Formulas crafted for the heart will often also include the fruits of hawthorn (*Crataegus*). Motherwort tincture can also be used to calm nervousness, ease the mind, and release tension.

Motherwort is beneficial in topical applications for minor wounds, rashes, or shingles. In these situations, the herb is applied directly to the area in a poultice, infused in water and used as a wash, or applied in an oil extraction as a salve, lotion, or balm.

◀ The pale pink to purple flowers of motherwort grow in whorl-like clusters along the stem.

MULLEIN

Verbascum thapsus

Common along roadsides, fields, and other open and sunny locations, the tall stalks of flowering mullein are a welcome sight to the artisan herbalist. This biennial member of the snapdragon family, *Scrophulariaceae,* is native to Europe, northern Africa, and Asia but was brought in the early 18th century to North America, where it quickly became widely established. Historically used as a dye plant and to craft torches and candlewicks, mullein has also long been considered a valuable addition to the herbal apothecary.

One of the earliest records of the medicinal benefits of *V. thapsus* comes from Greek physician, Pedanius Dioscorides, who wrote that the herb was useful for pulmonary diseases. This use has been echoed in numerous herbals over the years, and mullein is still prescribed for conditions of the lungs by modern practitioners. Indigenous North Americans took up the practice of smoking the leaves of the plant for this purpose, and many herbalists have experienced positive results with a tea brewed from mullein leaves to soothe a cough and ease congestion. It is important to note that any infusion of mullein leaves intended for consumption should be well filtered to remove all small "hairs," because they irritate the mouth and throat.

Many modern herbals recommend the use of mullein tincture, crafted from the leaves or roots of the plant, for respiratory complaints. Mullein root tincture is also known to be effective as an antispasmodic, which can be beneficial for back pain, muscle cramping, or even digestive issues.

Perhaps the most widely recognized use of *Verbascum thapsus* is as an infused oil for ear infections. For this application, it is the flowers of the herb that are infused in oil to be used as ear drops. The beautiful yellow flowers of mullein are harvested from second-year plants, and they should be allowed to wilt for a couple of hours to remove any moisture before being added to the oil. Mullein flowers have proven to be antibacterial as well as analgesic, and the infused oil can be used on minor wounds; it may also help ease the pain associated with arthritis, gout, and tired muscles.

◀ Delicate, yellow mullein flowers bloom along the stem of this beneficial biennial herb.

NETTLE

Urtica dioica

Any herbalist or forager who has stumbled into a patch of stinging
nettles will certainly remember this herb! A perennial plant native
to Europe and Asia, the stems and undersides of its leaves are covered in fine hairs, each tipped with histamine and other chemicals
that produce a stinging sensation and, in some cases, redness and
swelling. Despite this plant's effective self-defense, nettles have been
used for fiber, food, tea, and medicine since at least 1200 BCE.

It is always recommended that the artisan herbalist wear gloves when harvesting this herb to avoid being stung. The stinging action of *U. dioica* is neutralized by drying or heating the plant, so once the herb is processed, gloves are no longer necessary. This helpful plant is normally found growing in moist soils, along riverbanks, and in shady understories. Nettles are a nutritious spring green and can be harvested and dried to later be added to tea blends.

During the Roman conquest of Britain, soldiers would flog themselves with nettles before battle to increase alertness and energy. It's commonly thought that nettles will open the capillaries and stimulate the circulation, which would certainly give credence to this ancient practice. This herb has a long history of use as a topical treatment for joint pain and rheumatoid arthritis, and it is typically infused in oil for this purpose. *U. dioica* is considered anti-inflammatory, antibacterial, and astringent, and it can be used in a wide variety of skincare formulas. Oil infused with nettle leaf can be used directly on the afflicted area or crafted into a salve or lotion for ease of application.

An alcohol extract of nettle leaf was prescribed as early as the 1800s for patients suffering from anemia and chronic skin ailments, as well as urinary tract infections and kidney stones. Regular dosages of nettle tincture have shown promising results in the relief of the symptoms associated with seasonal allergies.

Nettle roots can be tinctured to be used as either a topical or internal treatment for joint pain. This tincture can be employed topically to relieve eczema, and on the scalp to reduce dandruff and stimulate hair growth.

◀ Pictured here is *U. dioica* subsp. *gracilis*. The serrated leaves and square stem of nettles conceal a stinging surprise!

PINE

Pinus spp.

There are over 100 species of evergreens in the genus *Pinus*, which are native to the Northern Hemisphere and found in a wide variety of environments. Pine trees are coniferous plants thought to have evolved nearly 95 million years ago. These species can be identified by their familiar cone as well as their leaves (needles), attached to the tree in bundles of two to five needles; the bundles are called *fascicles.* While the many species of Pine are certainly diverse, most of them have been utilized to some degree as a food source, and they are all considered valuable additions to the apothecary, with many overlapping benefits and uses.

Pine trees have been embraced by Indigenous cultures for a multitude of purposes, one of which is as a source of herbal medicine. The resin extracted from the tree, also known as *pitch,* can be infused in oil and made into a powerful salve for sore and achy muscles as well as an antimicrobial treatment for wounds, splinters, and insect bites.

The inner bark of pine can be harvested for its astringent and antimicrobial properties and brewed in a decoction to be used as a topical wash for a wide variety of skin ailments. Pine bark decoction can also be useful for treating coughs and other cold symptoms, while a tincture crafted from this inner bark has a long history of use easing stiff joints and relieving muscle pain when applied topically.

The needles of *Pinus* are high in vitamin C, and a tea brewed from these leaves is a traditional tonic against cold and flu. This tea is anti-inflammatory and a powerful expectorant that can offer relief from congestion and ease a cough. The artisan herbalist can also benefit from infusing pine needles in oil and crafting a balm to be used for itchy, dry skin as well as complaints resulting from topical inflammation.

◀ Needle clusters, bark and cones from two species of *Pinus:* red pine and white pine.

FUN FACT Although all species of pine produce edible seeds, culinary pine nuts are only harvested from pinyon pine varieties such as *Pinus edulis.*

PLANTAIN

Plantago spp.

Perhaps one of the most common "weeds" across the world, plantain is an inconspicuous herb that prefers to grow in open, sunny locations where the soil has recently been disturbed, but it can be found in parks, lawns, fields, and even growing through the cracks in broken sidewalks. Not to be confused with the Caribbean banana that shares the same common name, plantain has been a valued addition to the apothecary for hundreds of years.

Plantago major is native to most of Europe and Asia and was introduced into North America, where it quickly became naturalized, as did the narrow leaf plantain, *P. lanceolata*. Many modern herbals also include *P. rugelii* and *P. media*, which are both native to North America. Any of these species can be used interchangeably by the artisan herbalist.

A comparison of leaves from three species of plantain. From left: *P. major, P. lanceolata, P. rugelii.*

It's commonly thought that *Plantago major* is one of the nine sacred herbs mentioned in the *Lacnunga,* an Anglo-Saxon herbal written sometime in the 10th century. In this ancient tome, the herb was included as an ingredient in a salve prescribed for infections or inflammations of the skin. A more modern text, *The Book of Herbs,* written by Lady Rosalind Northcote in 1903, also includes plantain in an ointment to be used for burns or irritated skin.

Plantain is anti-inflammatory and antibacterial, so it is used in the healing of wounds. Modern practitioners recommend the herb for minor skin abrasions, bug bites, and insect stings. The fresh leaf can be chewed and applied to the affected area, or a salve can be crafted from plantain-infused oil for convenience of use when the fresh herb is not readily available. The herbalist should consider using *P. major* in any formulation designed to relieve itchy and irritated skin.

Teas brewed from the leaves of plantain have also been found to be effective for minor digestive complaints, hay fever, and sinus infections, as well as soothing a urinary tract infection. A tincture of plantain is known to ease a cough and could also be applied topically for its astringent qualities.

PURSLANE

Portulaca oleracea

The succulent leaves of purslane are no stranger to the gardener or forager. These resilient annual plants will grow in nearly any sunny location and are quite common garden weeds, but they will also thrive in poor, compact soils and willingly tolerate drought. The specific epithet, *oleracea,* loosely means "vegetable" or "herb of the kitchen," and purslane has been enjoyed as an edible green for hundreds of years, if not longer.

Thought to be native to the Indian subcontinent, purslane can now be found almost everywhere in the world. Although well established in North America, it is unknown how *P. oleracea* made its way here, but it is believed to have arrived pre-Columbian contact. Indigenous North Americans used this herb as a food, but they also used the leaves to make a soothing poultice for wounds and burns. They also brewed an infusion from the stems and leaves to relieve earaches.

This tasty and nutritious plant has been employed by herbalists for its cooling effect on the skin, where the succulent leaves are broken open and applied locally for burns, insect stings, and fevers. It is also used as a water infusion to aid digestion and to alleviate urinary complaints. In Europe, it is quite common to include purslane in cough syrup formulas, and the herb is also recommended to ease a headache.

When harvesting purslane, it's important to ensure proper identification of this useful plant. There is a common "look-alike" known as spurge (*Euphorbia*) that is toxic when consumed, but differentiating these two plants is quite easy to do. Purslane is a succulent with thick, fleshy stems and leaves (unlike spurge which has thin stems and paper-flat leaves). The leaves on *P. oleracea* grow in a slight whorl, while spurge leaves grow in opposite sets of two. Also, the stems of spurge when broken open will release a white sap, and purslane will not. The artisan herbalist must ensure proper identification of any herbs that will be harvested for use in the kitchen or apothecary.

◀ Purslane's succulent leaves make an excellent addition to soups, stews, and stir fry.

RASPBERRY

Rubus spp.

There are hundreds of species of *Rubus* distributed around the world, but fossil records dating back over 30 million years suggest that the genus originated in North America. The diversity of *Rubus* includes raspberry, blackberry, and dewberry, as well as hybrids such as loganberry, boysenberry, and tayberry. Many of these members of the rose family, *Rosaceae,* have been foraged and cultivated since antiquity, and the plants have been utilized by herbalists for millennia.

Although there are notable differences between species of raspberries and blackberries, many *Rubus* have been employed for similar medicinal uses, and there are numerous overlapping benefits throughout the genus. Around 400 BCE, the Greek physician Hippocrates recommended the leaves and branches of blackberry infused in white wine to be used as a poultice on wounds and during childbirth. In Dioscorides' book *De Materia Medica,* written between 50 and 70 CE, he suggests an infusion of raspberry leaf to be used topically for sores and insect bites, or drunk as a tea for digestive complaints.

Modern herbalists still recommend *Rubus* for many similar concerns. The leaves are cooling, toning, and astringent and can be brewed into a tonic for digestive issues, diarrhea, and stomach upset. Red raspberry leaf is a common ingredient in teas blended to relieve cramping related to menstruation and PMS. These teas are also good for relieving a sore throat and have been successful in stimulating the reproductive systems.

Raspberry and blackberry leaves can be infused in oil and crafted into topical products for conditions such as eczema or varicose veins. This treatment has also proven successful in reducing wrinkles, rejuvenating the skin, and protecting from UV damage. *Rubus* is also considered a beneficial ingredient in lotions or balms to soothe dry and cracked skin. A strong infusion of the leaves can be used as a wash to promote the health of hair and scalp.

◀ Flowers, leaves, berries, and brambles of raspberry and blackberry. Note the difference in thorns between raspberry (top) and blackberry (bottom).

RED CLOVER

Trifolium pratense

The dark pink flowers of this lovely herb are a common sight along roadsides and in fields and lawns and can be found growing in most parts of the world. Native to Europe, western Asia, and northwest Africa, this short-lived perennial is widely grown as a forage crop for cattle. Red clover is a member of the family *Fabaceae,* and is intentionally cultivated in many areas for its nitrogen-fixing qualities to improve farmland. The leaves and flowers of *T. pratense* are edible and can be enjoyed in salads or brewed into delicate and delicious teas.

Red clover was first brought to North America in 1663 to be used as a fodder crop but was quickly adopted by Indigenous populations that recognized its value as a medicinal herb. Brewed in a strong infusion and used as a topical wash, red clover was believed beneficial for inflammations of the skin such as eczema and psoriasis. The artisan herbalist could include red clover in a topical salve or lotion for these ailments, as well as to soothe burns and sores. Red clover demonstrates mild analgesic properties and can also be used to relieve sore muscles or arthritis pain.

Drunk as a tea, the infusion of red clover has shown promise for cough, asthma, and bronchitis. It is also widely believed that drinking red clover tea can purify the blood and detoxify the system. *Trifolium pratense* is used in traditional Chinese medicine for similar conditions and to cleanse the blood, release heat, and remove toxins.

Many modern herbals rightfully suggest the use of red clover tincture to boost the immune system, support lymphatic function, and as an internal treatment for psoriasis and eczema. The tincture has also shown to be beneficial in treating the symptoms of menopause, including fatigue, weight gain, and hot flashes.

The leaves of red clover can be easily recognized by the characteristic pale crescent on their outer half.

Women who are pregnant or breastfeeding should not consume medicinal doses of red clover as it may disturb important hormone balances.

ST. JOHN'S WORT

Hypericum perforatum

The golden, star-shaped flowers of this perennial herb tend to bloom around the summer solstice and the traditional Christian celebration of St. John the Baptist, which is where the modern common name of the herb originates. The genus name *Hypericum* is thought to come from the Greek and is a combination of the words "hyper," over or above, and "eikon," meaning picture or image. This likely refers to the traditional practice of hanging the plants on religious icons during the feast day celebrations. St. John's wort can be found growing in many open and sunny locations, including roadsides, meadows, and along the edges of woodlands. Native to Europe and Asia, *H. perforatum* has naturalized in temperate areas throughout the world and in some places is considered a noxious and invasive weed.

St. John's wort has been suggested as a treatment for depression dating back to ancient Greece, when it was prescribed to ease anxiety and improve the disposition. Some modern herbalists still recommend tea or tincture crafted from the aerial portions of the plant as an antidepressant, but it's important to note that St. John's wort interacts with a number of medications including oral contraceptives, heart and blood pressure medicines, as well as prescription antidepressants, so great care must be taken when considering *Hypericum perforatum* in this way.

Topical application of St. John's wort is a safe and effective method for the artisan herbalist to consider for a wide range of complaints. The herb is anti-inflammatory and antimicrobial. St. John's wort tincture is effective in treating minor wounds, burns, and inflammation of the skin.

Oil infused with the flowers of St. John's wort will take on a beautiful, deep red color due to the active constituent *hypericin*, which will also stain the herbalist's fingers during harvest. This infused oil is both nervine (beneficial to the nervous system) and analgesic and is specifically beneficial for neuropathy, shingles, sciatica, and other nervous system conditions. St. John's wort oil can be directly applied or crafted into a salve or lotion and is also useful for relieving muscle pain, arthritis, cramping, and sprains or bruising.

◀ A bowl of freshly harvested St. John's wort flowers is as beautiful as it is valuable to the Artisan Herbalist.

St. John's wort can interact negatively with heart and blood pressure medications as well as antidepressant medications, so it should not be taken internally in these cases.

WINTERGREEN
Gaultheria procumbens

The glossy green leaves and bright red berries of wintergreen can be found sprawling along the forest floor and in exposed mountainous areas throughout North America.

Spreading via underground rhizomes, this perennial evergreen grows low to the ground, most often in evergreen and hardwood forests. Wintergreen berries have a bright, minty taste and can be used to flavor an herbal tea blend or be added to foods. Sometimes called teaberry, this beneficial plant has been enjoyed as a flavorful edible herb for hundreds of years, and Indigenous populations also made use of wintergreen for its medicinal qualities.

Wintergreen leaves are high in tannins and are therefore astringent; this can be of benefit to the artisan herbalist when brewing a decoction intended to tighten and tone the body as well as for minor irritations and inflammations of the skin. The main chemical constituent of wintergreen is methyl salicylate, which is closely related to over-the-counter aspirin and therefore beneficial for pain relief, tired muscles, and similar complaints. In order to ensure proper extraction from the thick, glossy leaves of wintergreen, they must either be exposed to a long, slow decoction process or be allowed to steep in water anywhere from 12 to 24 hours.

Alternatively, the leaves can be processed in an alcohol extraction and the resulting tincture can be used. It's important to note that wintergreen tincture is a powerful medicine. It is *not* recommended for internal use—although it has been suggested for local application to relieve a toothache.

The aerial portions of *G. procumbens* can also be infused in oil, and this technique is possibly the most effective method for taking advantage of the medicinal virtues of this herb. Wintergreen-infused oil can be applied directly to the affected area, or salves and lotions can be made for ease of use and portability. The pain-relieving qualities of this oil can be quite useful for sore and tired muscles, joint pain, rheumatism, and arthritis. The oil is equally as effective for nerve pain, especially when combined with St. John's wort (*Hypericum perforatum*).

The glossy leaves of wintergreen, with their pale undersides, protect the small vibrant fruits.

Wintergreen essential oil is toxic and should never be consumed.

WITCH HAZEL
Hamamelis virginiana

A deciduous shrub (best known for the traditional use of its branches as a dowsing rod), witch hazel can be found growing along the edges of hardwood forests and near rivers and waterways. Although *H. virginiana* is native to the eastern half of North America, it has long been employed as a landscaping shrub and has been distributed throughout the continent and into Europe, where it can be found in yards, parks, and arboretums. There are three other species of *Hamamelis* native to North America, *H. mexicana*, *H. vernalis,* and the more recently discovered *H. ovalis*, although their natural distribution is more limited. In Asia, the artisan herbalist can find *H. japonica* and *H. mollis*. All of these species have been considered valuable as medicinal herbs, although the common American witch hazel is the most widely used.

Witch hazel leaves can be brewed into a tea, and this beverage is recommended for sore throats, diarrhea and cough. Externally, this same astringent infusion can be used for inflammations, varicose veins, and as a wash for minor injuries. A stronger brew is effective for poison ivy, eczema, and hemorrhoids.

A decoction of the bark and twigs of *H. virginiana* is quite beneficial as a facial cleanser due to its astringent and antibacterial qualities, and it is also known to be effective for acne, sunburn, insect bites, and bruising. After childbirth, many women use witch hazel-infused topical wipes for the herb's cooling and healing effect.

Commercial pharmacies offer a witch hazel product that is typically steam distilled from the bark of the shrub. This distillate is then combined with isopropyl alcohol as a preservative. The final product is significantly lower in tannins and other beneficial constituents when compared to a home-brewed witch hazel decoction. The leaves and twigs of witch hazel can also be tinctured at home and used in much the same way as its commercial counterpart, including as a spot treatment for acne and in a formula to promote oral health.

◀ The "nut" of the witch hazel tree is a capsule that contains two glossy-black seeds that are dispersed mechanically approximately eight months after flowering.

FUN FACT American witch hazel (*H. virginiana*) blooms in the fall, while vernal witch hazel blooms in late winter, and Asian varieties flower in the early spring!

YARROW

Achillea millefolium

The white flowers of yarrow bloom throughout the summer months and can be found along roadsides, in fields and meadows, and in many other locations that offer full sun and well-drained, sandy soil. Native to most of the Northern Hemisphere, this perennial herb spreads via underground rhizomes as well as by seed and can quickly overtake an area. Thankfully, this zealous herb is also highly valued in the apothecary and has been prized by herbalists for its healing qualities since antiquity.

It's said that Chiron the Centaur taught Achilles the healing power of yarrow, which he then used to heal his soldiers during war. The herb's specific epithet, *millefolium*, meaning "a thousand leaves," refers to the almost feather-like appearance of yarrow's leaf. In China, the dried stalks of yarrow have been used in correlation with the I-Ching for the purpose of divination, while the leaves and flowers have been employed for their astringent and styptic (blood-staunching) qualities. Similar to how yarrow was used in ancient Greece, the herb can be applied directly to a wound, or as a salve, to stop bleeding and to encourage healing. Yarrow is antibacterial and has been used to heal abrasions by herbalists around the world. This application is thought to be even more effective when the herb is combined with comfrey (*Symphytum officinale*).

Yarrow can be used topically for its mild analgesic quality and is often included in formulas for rheumatism. The fresh leaves can be chewed to help soothe a toothache, and a tea brewed from the leaves is known to bring relief from headaches.

Yarrow tea or tincture has shown to be helpful for reducing fever, encouraging sweat, and easing digestive discomforts. Crafted from either the leaves or flowers, these formulations have a long history of use treating cold and flu symptoms.

Oil infused with yarrow makes an excellent topical treatment for varicose veins and has often been found to help with hemorrhoids due to its astringent and anti-inflammatory qualities. A compress or poultice made from the freshly harvested herb would also be beneficial for these conditions. (A poultice is a topical application of herbs that have been macerated; a compress is a cloth or bandage moistened with an herbal infusion and applied to the skin.)

Women who are pregnant should not consume yarrow as it may stimulate uterine contractions.

◀ The composite structure of the yarrow inflorescence is a compact cluster of many individual flowers.

HERBS
FROM
THE
GARDEN

No MATTER the size of the garden bed, whether measured in acres or terra-cotta pots, tending the soil and cultivating our herbal allies from seed through harvest nurtures a deep connection between the medicine maker and their herbs.

BASIL

Ocimum basilicum

This flavorful herb loves warm weather and will perform best in a full-sun location. The fragrance of *O. basilicum* is reminiscent of black licorice, and the taste is bold and powerful. Widely utilized in Mediterranean food, basil is well known as the main ingredient in pesto and is one of the three ingredients of Caprese salad, a classic summer dish.

This member of the mint family is native to tropical regions, from Central Africa to Southeast Asia, and can easily be grown as an annual in any garden space providing partial to full sun and good drainage.

Basil has a long history of use in the apothecary as well as some interesting fables and folklore attached to it. In many cultures, including India, medieval Europe, and ancient Greece, basil was thought to be connected to the soul's passing into the afterlife. The Greek Orthodox Church uses this precious herb to sprinkle holy water during religious ceremonies.

◀ Traditional Genovese basil alongside a unique cultivar hybrid, *O. kilimandscharicum* x *basilicum,* African blue basil.

The species name *basilicum,* which comes from the Latin for "royal robes," is believed by some to be related to the mythological basilisk, a reptilian creature also known as the serpent king. It was commonly thought in medieval Europe that basil leaves left under a rock would transform into a lizard or that the smell of basil could, by itself, cause scorpions to grow in one's brain!

Despite this interesting and slightly frightening folklore, basil has been used for centuries by medicine makers for soothing the digestive system and calming muscle spasms as well as topically for insect and snake bites. This herb is considered to be anti-inflammatory and antibacterial.

Another well-known species of basil, *Ocimum tenuiflorum,* commonly referred to as tulsi or holy basil, is widely utilized for medicinal and therapeutic applications. This species has been documented in use for its calming and spiritual effects as early as 1000 BCE and is still enjoyed for these benefits today. Holy basil is considered to be an *adaptogen,* meaning that it helps the body adapt to various stress factors. It is also used for its anti-inflammatory benefits and support of the immune system.

CALENDULA

Calendula officinalis

The fiery bursts of color that calendula brings to the garden are reason enough to grow this beautiful member of the *Asteraceae* family. Originally domesticated in Europe, this helpful herbal ally is grown as a perennial in more mild climates but is often treated as an annual in areas that experience hard freezes or extended tropical heat.

While the most common *Calendula officinalis* plants will showcase orange or yellow blooms, there's a wide selection of varieties available with an assortment of blossom colors, all of which are valuable to the artisan herbalist.

Calendula has been included in gardens since at least the 12th century for both beauty and utility, and it has accumulated a fair share of folkloric uses and legends in that time. It was once thought that spreading calendula flowers under the bed would protect a house from robbery and that carrying calendula in one's pockets would ensure a positive outcome in a legal battle. Due to this perceived positive energy carried by the herb, it was often strung up as celebratory decorations and used as a garnish at important meals. The entire aerial portion of the plant is indeed edible, although the leaves are generally used in soups or stews since they aren't nearly as flavorful as the flowers.

Calendula's widespread use in commercial skincare products is likely due to the presence of the saponins, resins, and essentials oils contained within the flowers. The oils in the blooms are softening to the skin and aid in healing both abrasions and infections.

Simply harvesting the flowers on a sunny day will leave a gardener's hands feeling slightly sticky from the plant's plentiful essential oils. Calendula is well suited to both water and oil extractions. The herb is known to be astringent, antiviral, and anti-inflammatory, and, in alcohol extractions, *C. officinalis* it has also demonstrated antifungal properties.

It's also worth noting that calendula blossoms can be harvested for dye to be used in fabrics, foods, and cosmetic products. Considering the multitude of uses and benefits offered by this one flower, calendula is surely a "must-have" plant for every artisan herbalist.

◀ The many varieties of calendula create a stunning display in the herbalist's gardens.

CATNIP

Nepeta cataria

This short-lived perennial herb is a feline favorite and is commonly found in gardens—whether or not the gardener intended its inclusion. Catnip is a member of the mint family, as can be confirmed by the plant's square stem. It will happily grow in partial sun and is tolerant of transplanting. Once established in the garden, it can prove difficult to eradicate, but thankfully, *Nepeta cataria* also thrives when grown in containers.

Catnip is probably best known for its seductive and intoxicating effect on cats, but this attractant behavior only occurs with approximately two-thirds of felines; it depends on the cat's genetics. The herb is also very attractive to a number of different butterflies.

This herb is native to Europe, Africa, and Asia, and in medieval times catnip was thought to bring courage to those who chewed its roots. It was first introduced to North America sometime in the early 18th century; in 1712, a Massachusetts recipe included *N. cataria* as an ingredient for brewing ale.

Similar to other members of the mint family, *Lamiaceae*, catnip is quite often made into a tea for upset stomach and indigestion. Catnip tea was included in the 1735 *General Irish Herbal,* where it was prescribed for these ailments as well as to induce sweating and increase the appetite. The herb is also known to have a calming effect, especially on children, and it's widely employed for its efficacy as a mild sedative in tincture form.

One of the many beneficial qualities of catnip that deserves highlighting is its use as an insect repellent. The compound nepetalactone, which is thought to be the cat attractant in catnip, also repels flies, mosquitos, and other insects. A steam-distilled extract performs best as a spatial repellent, while a water or alcohol extraction is effective for topical application.

◄ Enjoyed by both herbalists and their feline companions, catnip is an elegant and useful addition to the herb garden.

CHAMOMILE

Chamaemelum nobile or *Matricaria chamomilla*

Chamomile is a name used to describe a handful of species in the plant family *Asteraceae*. Only two of the species are typically employed by the artisan herbalist for their benefits in the apothecary and in cosmetics. While these two plants are sometimes used interchangeably, they are distinctly different in growth habit as well as chemical constituents. *Chamaemelum nobile*, also known as Roman chamomile, is a low-growing, evergreen perennial while *Matricaria chamomilla*, German chamomile, is an upright herbaceous annual.

Roman chamomile is native to the UK and western Europe and, over time, it made its way into northern Africa and southwest Asia, while its counterpart originated in continental Europe and eventually traveled into western Asia. German settlers eventually brought *M. chamomilla* to North America, where it has become one of the most widely consumed commercially available herbal teas.

Chamomile is included in a number of topical skincare products for its emollient effect on the skin. Its anti-inflammatory benefits can be called upon to aid with dry, itchy, and hot skin conditions as well as insect bites, stings, and burns. This beneficial herb is anti-allergenic, antispasmodic, antibacterial, and antifungal.

Chamomile tea is widely enjoyed for its calmative effect. It's also regularly prescribed for stomach upset and irregularity. Chamomile is known to possess analgesic properties, and its use for rheumatic pain, arthritis, and back pain is well documented. For these purposes, the herb has been utilized in either a water or alcohol extraction for consumption or as a topical application dependent upon the ailment, the patient, and the herbalist's preferences.

It is important to note that people who are sensitive to ragweed, *Ambrosia artemisiifolia,* may also suffer allergic reactions to chamomile. While this is found to be the case most often with Roman chamomile, *C. nobile,* precautions should be taken with the use of any chamomile or other members of the Asteraceae family.

◀ Chamomile blossoms can be enjoyed either fresh or dried. Pictured here is German chamomile, *Matricaria chamomilla.*

COMFREY

Symphytum officinale

Comfrey is an herb of incredible value to the gardener, the medicine maker, and even to Mother Earth herself. If one only had space for a handful of useful plants, *Symphytum* should get a share of the garden plot! This perennial herb features a long, dark taproot that works its way deep into the soil, drawing up nutrients and minerals otherwise unreachable to most garden plants. The leaves make an excellent mulch and nutrient-dense compost, highlighting comfrey's utilitarian value. Gardeners growing in containers can simply harvest and process the entire plant while saving a piece of the rootstock to plant again.

This herb has been a star of the herbal apothecary for at least 2,000 years. It was included in Pliny the Elder's *Naturalis Historia,* which was published in 77 CE. In this ancient tome, comfrey was said to ensure the rapid healing of wounds, which is a purpose that the herb is still utilized for today.

Comfrey was also prescribed for this use in Dioscorides' *De Materia Medica,* which is the oldest herbal in Europe, having been published in 50 CE. Nicholas Culpeper continued this line of thinking in his 1656 work, *The English Physitian.* The herb's folk name, *knitbone,* alludes to comfrey's use in healing broken bones, and the herb has historically been used as a poultice for this exact purpose.

It is likely that all of these traditional texts are referring to the species *Symphytum officinale,* which is native to England and most of Europe. Many modern texts and herbalists in North America refer to a different species, *Symphytum × uplandicum,* or Russian comfrey, which is a hybrid cross between common comfrey and prickly comfrey. Russian comfrey was introduced to the UK around 1800 and was being shipped commercially to Canada by 1954. These two species are used interchangeably, but in laboratory testing, *S. officinale* has shown to be higher in the chemical compound allantoin. This compound is one of the chemicals believed responsible for comfrey's healing properties, as it stimulates the growth of new tissue; topical applications of comfrey are therefore quite beneficial for the healing of cuts, scrapes, and abrasions. It's important to note that this powerful herb is thought to be a potential carcinogenic, as well as hepatotoxic, when consumed, but topical application via tincture, poultice, or ointment is known to be safe and effective.

◀ The leaves and flowers of common comfrey. This beneficial herb is easy to grow and one of the Artisan Herbalist's most powerful allies.

ECHINACEA

Echinacea purpurea

Also known as purple coneflower, this beautiful herb is a lovely addition to any garden space. Echinacea is a perennial herb that happily reseeds itself, so a good-sized plot can be easily established in a short amount of time with very little effort. If only a small space is available, the best way to maintain echinacea is to harvest whole plants—roots and all—for use and then replant the crop again the next year. Growers who want to plant their echinacea crop annually should stratify the seeds to ensure good germination. This can be accomplished by simply sowing the seeds in the fall, or by refrigerating the seeds for a few weeks before planting in the spring.

The genus *Echinacea* gets its root from the classical Greek *echinos,* meaning "sea urchin" or "hedgehog," which refers to the bristly and round, dried seed head of the plants.

Echinacea is native to North America and has a long history of use amongst Indigenous populations; it is believed that the species *Echinacea angustifolia* was the most widely used. In Melvin Gilmore's 1914 book, *Uses of Plants by the Indians of the Missouri River Region,* he observed that echinacea was utilized for more ailments and conditions than any other plant available. Quite often, the root would be chewed to relieve toothaches, cough, and sore throat.

Modern studies have focused on the use of *E. purpurea* to boost the immune system and combat cold and flu. For these ailments, the roots and leaves can be employed in both tinctures and teas, although formulas that include the root are thought to be more medicinally beneficial. Both *E. angustifolia* and *E. purpurea* can be put to use by the artisan herbalist as well as *E. pallida,* the pale purple coneflower.

While the main focus of study has been on this plant's ability to boost the immune system, the herb also has a long history of topical use for burns, abrasions, swelling, bug bites, and other inflammation issues. Echinacea is well suited for use as a tincture, tea, or oil extraction for these conditions.

◀ Echinacea flowers bring a stunning splash of color and beauty to the herbalist's garden.

SAGE ADVICE To stratify echinacea seeds, simply mix them with moist peat moss or sawdust in a sealable baggie, and place it in the refrigerator for two to four weeks, to break dormancy.

HOREHOUND

Marrubium vulgare

The common horehound is a perennial member of the mint family, Lamiaceae. This herb is quite hardy, can tolerate cold temperatures, and will even thrive in poor soils. Like many of its mint relatives, horehound will spread easily when directly planted in the garden but can be contained by being grown in pots.

Horehound is native to Europe, northern Africa, and southwest Asia, and there are some differing ideas on where this square-stemmed herb first acquired its name. Some believe that horehound is named from a combination of the Old English words "hoar," for white or lightly colored, and "hune," a word referring to a class of plants. The other thought is that the plant acquired its name in ancient Egypt, where it was referred to as the "Seed of Horus." Regardless of where the herb was first named, it has historically been used to combat cold and flu symptoms and was most commonly prescribed for cough, fever, and mild pulmonary irritations.

The benefits of horehound can be harnessed for relief of cough, sore throat, and bronchitis. Herbal teas and tincture can be crafted from this useful herb, but the most common horehound medicines come in the form of syrups and cough drops. Horehound candies are widely available commercially, but they are very simple to produce in the home apothecary.

◁ The leaves of horehound are rough to the touch but release a mild, delicate fragrance when crushed.

HOREHOUND COUGH DROPS

1. Put the horehound leaves and water in a stainless steel saucepan and bring to the boil. Simmer for 20 minutes and then cool. Strain and squeeze out the herbs. Put the liquid back into the pan and add the brown sugar and the honey. While continually stirring with a wooden spoon, bring the liquid back to simmer. Continue stirring, and when the liquid falls from the spoon in a thread, test it by dropping a little into a cup of cold water. When your concoction is ready, the syrup will form hard, brittle threads. If you have a candy thermometer, check that the temperature reaches 295 to 309°F (146 to 154°C). If you overheat it and the mixture crystallizes, just add more water and a little more honey. When ready, pour the mixture into a lightly greased baking dish.

2. When cool enough, score the top to facilitate breaking the hardened mixture into squares or diagonals. Once broken up, shake icing sugar over the horehound cough drops to keep them from sticking together. Store in a glass jar.

> 1 cup of fresh or dried horehound
> 1 cup of water
> 2 cups of brown sugar
> 2 tbsp. honey
> Confectioner's sugar

HORSERADISH

Armoracia rusticana

This member of the Brassicaceae family is related to many familiar garden vegetables, including broccoli, turnips, and mustards. Horseradish is a perennial plant that's most well-known for the spicy condiment crafted from its root that is typically served with fish and other meats. *Armoracia rusticana* is a vigorous plant and can easily be grown from a piece of the harvested root, so even gardeners with limited space can enjoy this versatile medicinal herb. The herbalist should be aware that, due to its highly productive nature, horseradish can be quite challenging to fully remove from the garden once it has become well established.

Horseradish has been valued as a healing plant for well over 3,000 years, having been utilized in ancient Egypt as an aphrodisiac. The early Greeks used it for that purpose as well, but they also made use of the leaves and roots to prepare medicines to alleviate back pain, sore muscles, and even rheumatism. According to legend, the oracle at Delphi told Apollo that horseradish was worth its weight in gold!

Both the leaves and roots of the plant are of use to the artisan herbalist and can be used topically as a poultice or crafted into a salve for ease of application. In this way, horseradish can be of benefit for pain relief, whether from arthritic complaints or simply tired and sore muscles. There are a number of recipes in historic herbals calling for horseradish steeped in milk to be used on the skin. In these scenarios, the extraction is due to fat solubility, and therefore oil extractions would be just as effective.

Armoracia rusticana also has a history of use for sore throat, coughs, and fever. The herbalist can often prescribe a syrup or tea made from the leaves for these symptoms. A strong horseradish leaf tea with honey is a very powerful beverage for easing a cough.

While a tincture of horseradish may be too potent to ingest, it can certainly be considered for topical application. A number of traditional horseradish medicines are made from roots that are steeped in wine and are offered to the patient as a diuretic or to stimulate the digestive system.

◀ The roots, leaves, and flowers of horseradish offer a pungent flavor and aroma to any recipe.

Horseradish is not recommended for use during pregnancy or when breast-feeding due to potential toxic irritants in the root.

LAVENDER

Lavandula angustifolia

Lavender is a gorgeous, evergreen perennial plant that is commonly grown as an ornamental. It prefers full sun and well-drained soil and can easily be propagated by cuttings. In addition to its popularity as a decorative plant, lavender is also functionally useful as an ingredient in bath and body products as well as in the apothecary. The flowering spikes of this familiar herb are often harvested and bundled into sachets to freshen up the clothes drawer, or sewn into pillows to help the artisan get a good night's sleep.

Native to the Mediterranean region, *Lavandula angustifolia* has been prescribed medicinally for hundreds of years. It was included in Gerard's *Historie of Plantes* where it was said that an infusion of lavender flowers in distilled water or as an oil extract would aid in the treatment of palsy. This use for lavender was quite common, and can be found in many traditional herbal texts. Flowers of lavender were also infused in wine and either consumed or used topically to ease stiff joints and arthritis pain. A tincture of lavender flowers can be crafted by the artisan herbalist to ease similar complaints.

To this day, the most common use for lavender is as a relaxant, to calm the nerves and aid sleep. This has been accomplished by the use of tea (brewed from either the flowers or leaves of the herb) and even through the consumption of lavender tincture, although alcohol extracts of this plant are quite potent and are better suited to topical applications. Oils extractions of lavender in salves and lotions are also quite calming to the senses and can be used to relax the muscles and mind. Lavender is also beneficial for headaches, indigestion, and heartburn.

It is thought by some that lavender gets its name from the Old French *lavandre,* which is derived from the Latin *lavare,* which means "to wash." There are records of Romans using the flowers to scent their bathwater as well as the water used to wash their clothing. Lavender is antibacterial and anti-inflammatory. It has been prescribed for cuts and burns to relieve pain and disinfect wounds. Lavender essential oil was even used to clean hospitals during World War I.

A majority of the commercial production of lavender is for the production of essential oil, which is obtained through steam distillation of the flowers. Quite often, lavender grown for oil production is actually *Lavandula × intermedia,* also known as lavandin. This hybrid of *L. angustifolia* and *L. latifolia* has larger flowers and is easier to harvest than common lavender, but *L. angustifolia* remains the species preferred by the artisan herbalist.

◀ The fragrantly delicate flowers of lavender grow in whorls on spikes that rise above the foliage.

LEMON BALM

Melissa officinalis

This member of the mint family is easily recognized by its lemony fragrance and clean flavor. With small white flowers and opposite, light green leaves, lemon balm is an attractive addition to any garden space. This plant is a hardy perennial and can easily spread, so growers with limited available space might consider keeping their Melissa contained in a pot.

Lemon balm is native to southern Europe, where it was considered a near panacea in the apothecary. *Melissa officinalis* was so widely utilized that it quickly spread throughout the world. Lemon balm was held in such high esteem that in Culpeper's *Complete Herbal* of 1858, he stated that, "This herb is so well known to be an inhabitant in almost every garden that I shall not need to give any description thereof."

The name *Melissa* derives from the Greek word for honey bee, and *officinalis* refers to the herb's long history of use as an herbal medicine. For hundreds of years, lemon balm has been thought to relieve stress and to bring joy, and the herb is still commonly prescribed for this use. Studies have shown a notable tranquility in users that have consumed either tea or tincture prepared from the leaves. Ingestion of the tea is also linked to an improvement of mood and cognitive function, and, like other members of the mint family, lemon balm tea is useful for indigestion and stomach upset.

Lemon balm is also considered antiviral and antimicrobial. As a tea, the herb is a gentle yet potent medicine for fevers, colds, and flu. In tincture form, lemon balm has shown to be useful in combating cold sores and other viruses.

Topically, this wonderful herb can be useful for eczema and allergic reactions and as an aid in relief from insect bites and minor wounds. A water infusion may be employed for these types of ailments, but a salve or balm may prove to be more effective.

◀ The beautiful leaves of lemon balm exude a clean, lemony fragrance when crushed.

MINT

Mentha spp.

From candies and toothpaste, chewing gums, and alcoholic beverages, mint is a flavor that most everyone is familiar with. Typically, that crisp, cool taste is derived from an extraction of oils from one of two species of mint; *M. spicata,* commonly known as spearmint, or the hybrid *Mentha × piperita*, or peppermint. The well-known herb peppermint was derived from the hybridization of spearmint and water mint, *M. aquatica*. Hybridization is quite common amongst plants of the genus *Mentha*, resulting in the large number of hybrids and cultivars available today.

Most mint species have similar growing habits and spread quickly by underground stolons. This can be managed to a degree by growing mint in containers, but the gardener will find these plants quite eager to escape. Mints are incredibly hardy and will thrive in almost any condition, (although they prefer a moist and somewhat shady area), which makes them a perfect crop for the grower with limited space.

Many of the early recorded medicinal uses of mint refer to spearmint, which was recommended for settling an upset stomach, improving digestion, and soothing intestinal disorders. In 1801, Samuel Stearns' book *American Herbal* first promoted peppermint to relieve indigestion and flatulence. By the early 1900s, *M. × piperita* began to completely eclipse spearmint as an herbal remedy, and in modern herbals, it is almost exclusively peppermint that is suggested for use in the apothecary.

Small children should not drink peppermint tea because the high menthol content can be irritating to their respiratory systems. In these situations, the artisan herbalist can consider spearmint to be a viable alternative, as it contains noticeably less menthol than its counterpart. Spearmint's gentle nature also makes it suitable for topical use for itchy skin, rashes, and other irritations. Mint's antifungal qualities also lend quite well to use against athlete's foot and similar conditions.

◀ Freshly harvested mint leaves on display in a basket. This quickly spreading herb is cool and refreshing.

OREGANO

Origanum vulgare

Oregano is a familiar ingredient featured in many Italian dishes, and the flavor of this herb is peppery and warm. In the garden, *O. vulgare* is a sun-loving perennial that makes wonderful groundcover if allowed to spread. It's easily cultivated by cuttings and can be potted up and brought inside to enjoy all winter in areas that accumulate snow cover.

This herb is native to the Mediterranean region, where ancient Greeks thought it to be a useful antidote for poison and would use it topically to treat skin irritations and infections. By the 19th century, oregano was being prescribed as a tonic herb, and the plant was considered a panacea for a wide variety of ailments.

There are a number of cultivars of oregano available commercially, but the most prized is Greek oregano, *Origanum vulgare* var. *hirtum*. Suggested for both culinary and medicinal use, this variety has the highest concentration of volatile oils, hence the pungent aroma and flavor that this herb offers. Other species have been utilized in the apothecary over the years, including *O. onites*, which is also an antimicrobial, and *O. majorana,* the herb known as marjoram. While either of these species can be used by the artisan herbalist, they are not considered as potent as true oregano and therefore may not be as effective, depending on the usage.

Like other members of the mint family, oregano is useful to treat stomach upset, heartburn, and other digestive complaints. It is a handy remedy for coughs, sore throat, and even seasickness. Taken as a tea, oregano is warming and relaxing to the system. It has also shown to be of potential benefit for those who suffer from seasonal allergies.

Oregano is antimicrobial and can be employed topically to prevent infections. Traditionally, it has been used as a mouthwash for gum disease and tooth pain, and its analgesic properties would also lend themselves well to use in a topical salve. Additionally, this herb is antifungal and has long been recommended for use against candida, athlete's foot, and ringworm.

◄ Oregano is a fuzzy and flavorful herb that adds life to any recipe in the kitchen or apothecary.

SAGE

Salvia officinalis

Common garden sage is one of nearly 1,000 species of the genus *Salvia*. It is an herb that every artisan herbalist should be familiar with. This woody perennial thrives in full sun but will also tolerate life in a container indoors when placed in a south-facing window. These plants typically overwinter well in the garden, and one or two shrubs will produce enough harvestable leaves for anyone's household needs.

Sage is native to the Mediterranean region, and its name is thought to be derived from the Latin *salvere*, which means "to be healthy" or "to save." An old proverb asks, "Why should a man die, who has sage in his garden?" The specific epithet *officinalis* refers to a plant with commonly accepted medicinal uses. Sage has long been considered a tonic herb for a wide variety of ailments.

In John Gerard's 1597 book, *Historie of Plantes*, he claims that sage "is singularly good for the head and brain, it quickeneth the senses and memory." For hundreds of years, *Salvia officinalis* has also been prescribed for insect bites, nervous conditions, hair care, oral health, and as a local anesthetic.

Modern herbalists still employ the use of sage leaf infusion as a mouthwash and gargle for general oral health, as well as for infections and sore throats. For sore throats, blending the infusion with vinegar before gargling is generally found to be even more effective. Sage tea is also beneficial for fever, cough, and digestive issues. When consumed in small and frequent doses, consumption of sage tea is found to improve cognitive function and aid memory.

S. officinalis can be used topically to cleanse and heal skin abrasions, and, as a salve or tincture, the herb has shown great benefit for those who suffer from eczema, psoriasis, and acne. A lotion crafted from the leaves of sage could be used to address stretch marks and swelling or to simply provide relief from dryness and irritation.

Another species of sage that has gained mainstream popularity in recent years is white sage, *S. apiana*. While the two species are not interchangeable in the apothecary, white sage is still an herb that the artisan herbalist should consider for further study. It grows wild in the southwestern part of the United States and northwestern Mexico and has long been used as a ceremonial and sacred herb by Indigenous populations. However, due to the increasing popularity of using white sage for smudging (the Indigenous practice of burning an herb to cleanse or purify a person or space), wild stands of this herb have been overharvested, and the future survival of this important herb is a concern.

◀ The textured, rugose leaves of sage release their pungent aroma when crushed.

SAGE ADVICE Ethical harvesting of wild plants is a critical practice. We must make an effort to be sure that future generations can also have the opportunity to work with these herbal allies that provide us with our food and medicine.

THYME

Thymus vulgaris

The small, tubular flowers of common garden thyme are very attractive to the bees that create delicious and delicate honey from its nectar. A perennial herb native to the western Mediterranean, *T. vulgaris* loves to grow in full sun and high heat and is very tolerant of drought. The plant can be propagated by seed, cuttings, or root division and easily handles a hard freeze, making this one of the easiest plants for a gardener to maintain.

It's widely thought that thyme gets its name from a combination of the Greek words *thumos,* for smoke and *thyo,* which means sacrifice. The herb was often burned as incense throughout ancient Greece, particularly in temples and during important ceremonies. In the first century BCE, the Roman poet Virgil stated that this pungent herb, when combined with garlic, would combat fatigue.

◄ Despite the minuscule size of its leaves and flowers, thyme is a powerful herbal ally.

Like many other members of the mint family, thyme infusion has been used to alleviate stomach upset and digestive complaints. It's also quite beneficial for sore throat, and thyme tea is well known to help eliminate a cough. Topically, when applied to the chest and back as a salve, thyme is a powerful expectorant. The salve also offers mild analgesic properties, and it can be employed for the relief of joint pain and arthritis.

One of the most beneficial constituents of *Thymus vulgaris* is thymol, which gives the herb its distinctive flavor and aroma. Thymol is a potent antiseptic, which is why this herb has been used on skin infections and minor wounds, as well as in mouthwashes for oral ailments and gingivitis. Thymol is the active ingredient in a number of commercially available mouthwashes and sanitizer products.

Although thymol is slightly water-soluble and can be harnessed to some degree in a water extraction, it is much better for the artisan herbalist to consider alcohol or oil extractions when hoping to take advantage of thyme's antiseptic properties.

THE
SPICE
RACK

REGARDLESS OF the season, the artisan herbalist needs to look no further than their own kitchen for an abundant selection of healing herbs, seeds and spices. The culinary spice rack offers numerous ingredients well suited for use in various medicinal formulations.

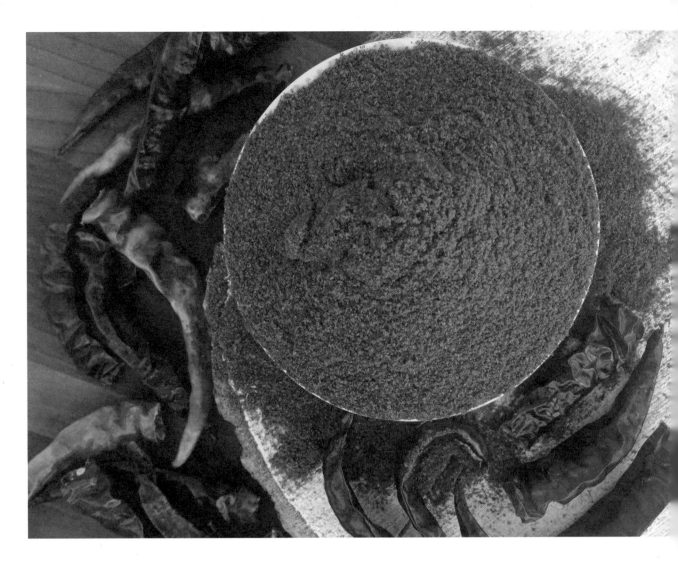

CAYENNE

Capsicum annuum

An old standby in most spice racks is the bottle of spicy goodness labeled "crushed red pepper flakes." These containers are typically filled with *Capsicum annuum,* a hot pepper known as cayenne, which is just one of the many species of pepper. Cayenne is believed to have originally been domesticated in the area now known as Mexico nearly 6,500 years ago, and there are currently hundreds of recognized cultivars. This beneficial spice can also be grown at home with ease; the ripened pods can be enjoyed in both the kitchen and the apothecary.

Cayenne is a moderately spicy variety, with a typical Scoville rating of 30,000 to 50,000 units. While the Scoville scale is an imperfect system for calculating the heat of any given *Capsicum*, the ratings give the artisan herbalist a general idea of the levels of capsaicin present in the fruit. Capsaicin is the active component of chili peppers; it's what creates the burning sensation we experience when consuming the pods, but it is also the chemical responsible for many of the medicinal uses of this potent plant species. While cayenne is usually the variety used in the apothecary, any member of the *C. annuum* species with a similar Scoville rating can be substituted, if necessary.

This spice has a history of use for stimulating the digestive system, either through inclusion in a meal or as an ingredient in an herbal tea blend. It is thought by many traditional healers that adding cayenne to a medicinal brew will help the body digest and process the herbs more quickly. Cayenne is a warming herb that will induce a sweat, so it is often recommended to help alleviate cold and fever.

C. annuum stimulates the cardiovascular system and improves circulation. It has long been considered useful in alleviating and toning a sluggish system. Topically, cayenne can be employed for its analgesic properties in a salve or lotion to relieve arthritis complaints and to soothe sore and tired muscles. If possible, the artisan herbalist should always consider the addition of cayenne in formulas for this purpose.

This spice is also noted to be antimicrobial and antibacterial and can be used topically as a spot treatment for acne and to help bring relief from the effects of poison ivy.

◀ Whether crushed, powdered, dry or fresh, cayenne pepper is a versatile spice that will add a potent heat to any formulation.

FUN FACT Pharmacologist William Scoville invented the Scoville Scale in 1912 as a method to measure the heat of *Capsicum* peppers. This scale is the standard still used today to describe the spiciness of a variety.

CINNAMON

Cinnamomum verum

One of the oldest-recorded spices, cinnamon has a long and mysterious history. It was imported into Egypt as early as 2000 BCE and was so highly prized that it was considered only fit for use by royalty or to be offered as gifts to the gods. The source of this precious spice was kept so secret by traders that the origins of the strongly scented bark remained a mystery until around 1270 CE, when it was revealed in Zakariya al-Qazwini's geographical dictionary, *Monument of Places and History of God's Bondsmen,* that cinnamon was grown in Sri Lanka.

Today, a majority of the commercial cinnamon available is actually *C. cassia,* also known as Chinese cinnamon. As the name implies, this species is native to China and is often referred to as simply cassia. It is considered of lesser quality than the true cinnamon from Sri Lanka and India. There are a handful of other species available, including *C. burmannii,* from Indonesia, *C. loureiroi,* the Vietnamese cinnamon and *C. citriodorum* from Malabar. While all of these species of *Cinnamomum* have been used by herbalists over the years, and each offers similar benefits, the true cinnamon, *C. verum,* is recommended for use whenever possible. Cinnamon contains a chemical compound called coumarin, which, in high doses, can be toxic to humans. Studies have shown that true cinnamon, *C. verum,* is significantly lower in this compound than its counterparts, and therefore it is much safer to consume in larger doses.

Cinnamon can be included in tea blends to aid in digestion or to add a warming effect to a brew. The spice is stimulating and promotes good circulation. It has a long history of use for alleviating sore throat and relieving cough.

It has also shown to be antibacterial, antifungal, and antiviral. Topically, oil infused with cinnamon can be used for arthritis, muscular pain, and similar ailments. There are a number of beneficial folk remedies that include cinnamon for hair loss, acne, and eczema.

◄ The curled bark of the cinnamon tree is a warm and comforting spice that can be used either in its whole form or ground into a powder.

Women who are pregnant or breastfeeding should not consume medicinal doses of cinnamon as it may disrupt glucose regulation or cause uterine contractions.

CLOVES

Syzygium aromaticum

Cloves are the unopened flower buds of an evergreen tree native to Indonesia. Probably most widely recognized as a flavor in holiday desserts, this aromatic spice is also commonly used as an addition to cigarettes, and, stuck into citrus fruits, it is part of an insect-repelling pomander. As one of the plants included in the ancient spice trade, *S. aromaticum* has a significant history of use in the kitchen as well as in the apothecary.

The name *clove* comes from the French word for nail, likely attributed to its shape, but the plant didn't even reach Europe until the 4th century BCE. Before that time, the spice had been used medicinally in China and India for hundreds of years to strengthen the immune system, as a digestive aid, and for its anti-inflammatory properties.

Cloves are considered analgesic, anti-inflammatory, antiviral, and antimicrobial. They have been used topically (generally in an oil infusion or in products crafted from these oils) for a number of skin conditions, irritations, and for pain relief. The spice has proven effective as a spot treatment for acne; it also stimulates the circulation and tightens and tones aged skin.

Tinctures and salves crafted from clove buds have also shown to be beneficial in alleviating arthritis pain, and clove massage oil brings a warming and welcome relief to tired and sore muscles.

The fragrance of cloves is thought to calm the mind and reduce stress, and a small amount of this spice in an herbal tea blend is sure to aid in that endeavor. The flavor of cloves is spicy and comforting.

The use of the dried *Syzygium aromaticum* in a pomander to repel insects is well merited and, whether through decoction or infused oil, the spice can certainly be included in the artisan herbalist's formulas for this purpose.

◄ The small buds of cloves are a familiar addition to many holiday recipes, but this flavorful spice is well suited to the herbal apothecary.

SAGE ADVICE Crafting a homemade pomander is easy! Simply pierce a firm orange with a toothpick or needle and insert the clove bud into the hole. Repeat in any pattern desired until the majority of the fruit is covered. Decorate and hang with a ribbon, if desired.

GARLIC

Allium sativum

Sometimes referred to as the stinking rose, due to its pungent aroma, garlic is a spice that has been enjoyed in both the kitchen and the apothecary for over 4,000 years. Thought to have originally been cultivated in Mesopotamia, this spicy root was even found well preserved in the tomb of the famous King Tut, who died sometime around the year 1325 BCE. By the 2nd century, garlic was documented by herbalists as useful for such a wide variety of ailments and conditions that it could easily be considered a medicinal panacea.

When raw garlic is chopped, crushed, or chewed, it produces a compound known as allicin. This compound is thought to be the cause of the spicy flavor of the root as well as a large part of its medicinal value. Cooking will destroy allicin, so the use of raw garlic is recommended for medicinal applications. While laboratory studies have been inconclusive, there is much anecdotal evidence to support the traditional use of garlic in battling the symptoms of the common cold, which may partly be due to the spice's high zinc content.

Garlic is considered to be antiseptic, antimicrobial, and antiviral and has been used topically for numerous conditions, although many people can be sensitive to the direct application of raw garlic on the skin. In many cases, the artisan herbalist can employ garlic-infused oil for topical use to treat fungal infections such as athlete's foot or as a circulatory stimulant. It is thought that this oil could be effective for psoriasis, acne, or the reduction of scarring.

Traditionally, garlic has also been used to support cardiovascular health. It has been prescribed for use in herbal teas as well as regular inclusion in meals. While clinical testing is just beginning to reveal the extent of this plant's usefulness in the apothecary, it has remained highly recommended by herbalists since its earliest mentions in classical herbal texts.

◀ The spicy bulbs of the garlic plant are pungent and flavorful. This spice should be considered one of the most beneficial allies of the Artisan Herbalist.

GINGER

Zingiber officinale

Ginger is a spice that has been valued and traded since antiquity. This flavorful rhizome is thought to have originated in the islands of Southeast Asia and was domesticated for cultivation over 5,000 years ago. From its homeland, it made its way to China, where it was included in Emperor Shen Nong's herbal, *Sheng Nong Ben Cao Jing*, around 2000 BCE. We see ginger mentioned again 1,600 years later, in the Sanskrit texts of India, and within a few centuries this ancient spice had become wildly popular throughout the Roman Empire. *Z. officinale* wasn't just prized as a spice; it was also widely utilized in the apothecary.

This relative of turmeric and cardamom has been used by artisan herbalists for thousands of years for its warming and stimulating effects. Long thought to be an aphrodisiac, it has been suggested as an addition to foods, as a tea, and as a topical ointment for this purpose. Ginger infused in oil can be applied topically to stimulate the circulatory system and encourage blood flow and is also found to be useful for cramping and sore muscles. This oil can also be used directly or crafted into a salve or lotion to help with rheumatoid and osteoarthritis.

Historically, ginger has been prescribed for issues of the heart, lungs, and stomach. Perhaps one of the most well-known modern uses of the spice is for alleviating nausea. *Zingiber officinale* is known to stimulate the appetite, aid in digestion, and alleviate heartburn and stomach upset. These effects are best achieved by drinking ginger tea, which is also a potential remedy for sore throat. The artisan herbalist can choose to employ a tea that is exclusively ginger, or a blend of healing herbs.

It is thought by many that fresh ginger is preferred over dried when used to relieve nausea, but in many situations the two can be used interchangeably by the artisan herbalist, depending on the need and what is available.

◀ The rhizomatous ginger is a classic herbal ally and can be enjoyed in its whole form or dried, ground, or powdered.

Large quantities of ginger are not recommended for consumption during pregnancy as this may increase the risk of miscarriage.

TURMERIC

Curcuma longa

This brightly colored rhizome is in the same family as ginger, *Zingiberaceae,* and has been prized by herbalists for nearly as long as its better-known cousin. The genus name *Curcuma* is thought to come from the Sanskrit *kuṅkuma,* which referred to both turmeric and saffron, both of which have been used for millennia to imbue foods and fabrics with a beautiful golden color. Native to the Indian subcontinent, turmeric has been used as a flavoring as well as a dye, and it has been in the apothecary for nearly 4,000 years.

Much like its cousin, turmeric has been used to aid in digestion, stimulate the appetite, and soothe an upset stomach. Its bitter flavor lends itself well to use as a digestive aid, and this spice is also helpful in stimulating the liver and gallbladder. Turmeric has a wide history of use for topical skin conditions, including burns, cuts, bruising, and rashes. This is likely due to the rhizome's antiseptic and antibacterial qualities. There are a number of commercial face creams on the market that are crafted with turmeric.

Long considered an anti-inflammatory, there are numerous traditional and modern formulas that use turmeric for this purpose. One of the active chemical constituents of the spice is curcumin, which is what gives the rhizome its color and what is thought to be its main medicinal component. It's important to note that curcumin is not water-soluble, so the use of turmeric in herbal tea will not be as effective as a tincture or oil-based preparation. Turmeric tinctures are well suited to topical applications, as are salves or balms crafted from the spice.

The artisan herbalist can also make use of the fat-soluble nature of curcumin by brewing the ancient tonic beverage known as golden milk. This flavorful drink has been used by traditional medicine makers for centuries, and the formula is simple enough that anyone can enjoy its warming flavor and healing properties at home. Traditionally, the recipe for golden milk has also included black pepper (*Piper nigrum*), as it's believed to help the body absorb the medicinal qualities of the drink and increase its efficiency. (The full recipe is given in Section Three.)

> Medicinal doses of turmeric are not recommended for consumption during pregnancy as it may cause complications.

◀ With its intense orange color and warming spice, turmeric will add intense layers of depth to any recipe or herbal formulation.

3

RECIPES AND FORMULAS

TEAS

CALMING TEA

Sitting back with a warm, soothing cup of tea is the perfect way to relax. This herbal blend will help ease stress, encourage peace of mind, and aid relaxation.

1. Combine herbs and place in a reusable tea bag or tea ball. Heat water until just boiling. Pour it over herbs and let steep for 5–7 minutes. Enjoy with honey.

> 2 parts chamomile
> 2 parts lemon balm
> 1 part red clover
> Pinch of lavender or clove
>   buds to taste.

UPLIFTING TEA

Sometimes a hot cup of tea is just what's needed to reboot and recharge the system. This blend of uplifting herbs will invigorate the body and mind.

1. Combine herbs and place in a reusable tea bag or tea ball. Heat water until just boiling. Pour it over herbs and let steep for 5–7 minutes. This tea is warming and energizing and is quite enjoyable with a splash of milk.

> 2 parts nettle leaf
> 1 part calendula
> 1 part oregano
> Cinnamon to taste

FOCUSING TEA

2 parts sage
1 part rosemary
1 part peppermint
1 slice fresh ginger root

When the mind wanders and the herbalist is easily distracted, a cup of tea may be all that is needed to bring focus and clarity. This blend stimulates cognitive function and improves memory.

1. Combine herbs and place in a reusable tea bag or tea ball. Heat water until just boiling. Pour it over herbs and let steep for 5-7 minutes. This delightful brew is enjoyable hot, but can also be made into a delicious iced tea.

IMMUNI-TEA

2 parts nettle leaf
2 parts echinacea
1 part elderflower
1 part sage
1 part pine needles
Ginger root

Whether as a preventative or to help ease symptoms, a cup of herbal tea can be an enjoyable way to battle the effects of a cold and boost the immune system.

1. Combine herbs and place in a reusable tea bag or tea ball. Heat water until just boiling. Pour it over herbs and let steep for 5-7 minutes. This tea is warming as well as delicious. Although beneficial during cold and flu season, this brew is an enjoyable beverage all year long.

HEART-HEALTHY TEA

This herbal tea blend supports heart health and is a flavorful way to strengthen and tone the cardiovascular system.

2 parts hawthorn
1 part raspberry leaf
1 part sage
1 part wintergreen

1. Combine herbs and place in a reusable tea bag or tea ball. Heat water until just boiling. Pour it over herbs and let steep for 5–7 minutes. Enjoy this tea with a spoonful of honey.

TINCTURES

ANTI-INFLAMMATORY TINCTURE

This is a potent extraction of herbs to relieve inflammation. The herbs can be combined and tinctured at a ratio of 1:3, or tinctured individually at the ratios listed below and then blended.

2 parts nettle leaf (1:2)
1 part basil (1:2)
1 part turmeric (1:5)

1. Tincture the herbs as described in Section One, "Crafting the Tincture." Use 15–30 drops a day, up to four times a day, as needed.

DAILY TONIC TINCTURE

A daily tonic will revitalize the body and mind. The herbs can be combined and tinctured at a ratio of 1:3, or tinctured individually at the ratios listed here and then blended.

1 part dandelion root (1:3)
1 part red clover (1:2)
1 part rosemary (1:2)
1 part lemon balm (1:3)

1. Tincture the herbs as described in Section One, "Crafting the Tincture." Use 20–30 drops a day, as needed.

IMMUNE BOOST TINCTURE

An immune-boosting tincture will serve as a powerful preventative against cold and flu. The herbs can be combined and tinctured at a ratio of 1:3, or tinctured individually at the ratios listed here and then blended.

2 parts elderflower (1:4)
1 part echinacea root (1:3)
1 part sage (1:3)

1. Tincture the herbs as described in Section One, "Crafting the Tincture." Use 10–15 drops a day, up to four times a day, as needed.

CALMING TINCTURE

The relaxing blend of herbs in this tincture will help calm the mind and lift the spirits. The herbs can be combined and tinctured at a ratio of 1:3, or tinctured individually at the ratios listed here and then blended.

2 parts motherwort (1:3)
1 part lavender leaf (1:4)
1 part lemon balm (1:3)

1. Tincture the herbs as described in Section One, "Crafting the Tincture." Use 15–30 drops a day, up to four times a day, as needed.

OILS

SORE MUSCLE SALVE

This basic recipe is a perfect blend of herbs for topical treatment of sore and tired muscles.

1. Combine equal parts of both ingredients and infuse in oil of choice for 4–6 weeks. Process as described in Section One of this book, "Crafting a Salve." Use topically as needed.

1 part cayenne peppers
1 part wintergreen leaves

ARTHRITIS RELIEF SALVE

An herbal blend designed to bring relief from inflammation, joint pain, and arthritis.

1. Combine ingredients and infuse in oil of choice for 4–6 weeks. Process as described in Section One of this book, "Crafting a Salve." Use topically as needed.

2 part nettles
1 part cayenne
1 part witch hazel
1 part turmeric

BUG BITES AND BOO-BOOS SALVE

1 part comfrey

1 part yarrow

1 part chickweed

1 part plantain

This salve is a topical ointment for healing minor abrasions, skin irritations, and insect bites.

1. Combine ingredients and infuse in oil of choice for 4–6 weeks. Process as described in Section One of this book, "Crafting a Salve." Use topically as needed.

HEALING LOTION FOR DRY SKIN

1 part dandelion flower

1 part plantain leaf

1 part chamomile flower

1 part lavender flower

The oil in this recipe is infused with a healing blend of herbs, creating a soft and soothing lotion for overly dry or mildly irritated skin.

1. Combine ingredients and infuse in oil of choice 4–6 weeks. Strain infused oil and craft lotion as described in Section One of this book, "Crafting a Lotion." Enjoy.

MOISTURIZING LIP BALM

An easy-to-craft lip balm that contains an herb-infused oil designed to moisturize and heal dry, chapped lips.

1. Combine ingredients and infuse in oil of choice 4–6 weeks. Strain infused oil and craft lip balm as described in Section One of this book, "Crafting a Lotion." Pour into individual lip balm tubes and enjoy.

2 parts calendula flower
1 part chamomile flower
1 part either lemon balm or lavender

RELAXATION MASSAGE OIL

Massage oil designed to ease the muscles and relax the mind.

1. Combine ingredients and infuse in oil of choice for 4–6 weeks. This massage oil can be applied directly to the skin. Consider the addition of ginger or cayenne for a warming, anti-inflammatory blend.

1 part st. John's wort flowers
1 part wintergreen leaves
1 part lavender flowers

MISCELLANEOUS

HERBAL SUGAR SCRUB

Sugar scrubs are simple products to create, and infusing the oil in the recipe with beneficial herbs will give these scrubs the added boost they need to really stand out in a shower routine.

You can use lavender for a calming oil for sensitive skin, calendula for a soothing and moisturizing oil, or peppermint to create an invigorating oil for tired muscles.

1 cup granulated sugar
¾ to 1 cup herb-infused oil

1. Infuse oil with chosen herbs for two weeks. Combine sugar and infused oil. Mix well. Store scrub in a screw-top glass jar. Enjoy.

GOLDEN MILK

This traditional Indian beverage is delicious and loaded with anti-inflammatory spices.

3 cups milk (or non-dairy alternative)
1½ tsp. ground turmeric
1 tsp fresh sliced ginger root
1 cinnamon stick
¼ tsp. whole black peppercorns

1. Heat the milk in a saucepan over low heat. Once warm, add spices and slowly simmer until hot, approximately 5 minutes. Avoid bringing milk to boil. Strain and serve. Makes 2 servings.

BASIC HERBAL SYRUP

Whether employed as a medicinal dose or included in cocktails, syrups are a great way to utilize the many benefits of herbs. This basic recipe can be used with any herb or combination of herbs.

1 oz. herbs
16 oz. of water

1. Bring to boil and simmer until liquid is reduced by half. Strain herbs and combine the liquid with honey at a 1:1 ratio for optimal shelf life. Store in refrigerator. If the syrup is too sweet, use less honey.

TO DO.

- [ ] Logo
- [ ] Mission statement
- [ ] Social media
- [ ] Website

4

BUILDING AN HERBAL BUSINESS

WHILE SOME PEOPLE are perfectly content crafting healthy herbal products just for themselves—and maybe their family and friends—other herbalists may decide to take their knowledge and skills on a more entrepreneurial route and go into business for themselves. Both paths can be rewarding and empowering, but anyone interested in building an herbal business will achieve greater success through proper planning and execution of their herbal dreams. Remember, most people study for many years before feeling ready to launch an herbal business. For your own happiness and the safety of your clients, practice patience and don't rush yourself to get your business established.

DEVELOP YOUR BRAND

When you are ready to turn your herbal studies into a business, the first step will be developing your brand, or your image. How do you want the world to see you and your herbal products? Sit down and make a list of what you hope to offer to the world: what is your mission? Is it simply to make enough money to help cover the cost of your herbal hobby, or are you hoping to build a brand large enough to be offered in grocery stores and pharmacies across the country? Be honest with yourself, and write down everything relevant that comes to mind. This information will be useful later when you venture out into the world as a new business owner. Make a point of reviewing this list from time to time so you don't lose sight of what's important in the day-to-day struggle of building your business into a profitable venture. Your list will be your guide as you develop your company's mission statement, defining your business's goals and values.

The identity that you create for your business will be molded by this list of your values, dreams, ambitions, and goals. As this new identity takes shape, it will express itself in your mission statement, your packaging, and your logo. Speaking of logos: are you going to design your own or hire a graphic designer to create this very important piece of your branding puzzle? If you have the skills and computer programs necessary to design a high-quality logo that truly represents your business and message, then you're a step ahead of most! Otherwise, it's wise to hire a professional. Your logo is the world's first impression of your new business, so, if you are planning to grow your customer base beyond just your family and friends, consider investing in a professionally designed logo; it will pay for itself in no time.

BUSINESS GOALS

As you work to formulate your brand and mission as a new herbal entrepreneur, you'll need to define your future business goals. Do you hope that your new business will grow into full-time employment, or are you happy keeping it as a "side hustle"? Do you imagine selling direct to the consumer, or do you prefer a wholesale model? Don't worry, none of these decisions are cast in stone—your goals and plans will evolve over time as you become more experienced in the field. It's important, though, to work through these ideas and find a comfortable place for yourself within the herbal wellness market.

SOURCING YOUR HERBS AND OTHER INGREDIENTS

One of the most important decisions to be made when creating herbal products, whether commercially or for home use, is which source(s) of herbs to use. The quality of your ingredients determines the quality of your final products, and ideally, the artisan herbalist is dedicated to providing high-quality herbal preparations. When sourcing herbs, the responsible herbalist will choose ingredients that are as close to their natural source as possible, whenever possible. In Section Two of this book, we learned about harvesting herbs from one's local environment, growing herbal gardens of various sizes, and looking to the kitchen for medicinal herbs and spices that are typically viewed as strictly culinary ingredients. If none of these options are available to you, it is certainly possible to purchase herbs from a local co-op, grocery, or even online stores. Regardless of how the herbalist acquires their herbs, if the decision is mindful and care is taken to use the highest-quality ingredients possible, then the herbalist can rest at ease knowing they have done the best they can with the resources available to them.

PACKAGING

Which packaging to use for a line of herbal products is another decision that will be heavily influenced by the scale of the business model you have created. There are many bottle and container companies online, and browsing through their available options is a great way to get a feel for the style and design of packaging you might find suitable. The herbalist will need to weigh the pros and cons of the various packaging materials and decide if they prefer glass, metal, or plastic containers. If plastic is the chosen material, it may need to be food grade or BPA-free, depending on its anticipated use.

Of course, the larger the quantity of bottles or containers that the herbalist purchases at a time, the lower the price per item will be, so be direct and honest with yourself about what you can afford, and what kind of sales numbers you can expect when you roll out your new product line. If you can make the investment in larger quantities now and can justify this outlay with projected sales, this will give you a good head start toward profitability by helping you keep costs down. Packaging can be one of the biggest expenses the herbalist will need to account for in their pricing model.

Because of the nature of your product, containers may need to be sealed. This is especially true for tins, jars, or bottles that contain liquids. The herbalist will need to price the appropriate materials and equipment for sealing their containers, including the heat shrinkable bands used for this task. Something as simple as a handheld hairdryer will work for sealing a small number of containers, but upgrading to a heat gun is a worthwhile investment that should be considered early on.

The artisan herbalist may also need to purchase additional equipment when crafting products on a larger, commercial scale. This could include a double boiler, bowls, scales, funnels, and various other items, all of which will need to be factored into the startup budget.

LABELING

Once the herbalist has developed the recipes, created the products, and chosen the packaging, the next order of business is designing and printing labels. This part of the process involves a handful of important decisions. The design of the label needs to appeal to customers, and it must also convey what your product does and why it's a better choice than any other. Will you be designing your labels yourself or hiring a professional? Will you be printing the labels yourself, or will you pay a local or online printer to handle this job? To make these decisions, the herbal entrepreneur once again needs to evaluate their goals for the scale of their operation and plan accordingly. It's always better to start small and keep things simple when first starting out. As your business develops, you'll have a better idea of what works for you and what doesn't. While we may have big dreams when we first enter the business world, these can quickly evolve once we've gained more experience in the field. This is perfectly normal and to be expected. Don't hold on to your initial dreams too tightly; allow them to adjust as you find your niche in the market.

Example of a product label including key components such as: 1) ingredients list, 2) volume or weight of product, 3) slogan or tagline, 4) significant features of the product, and 5) website and contact information.

PRICING

One of the greatest downfalls to plague a new business is a pricing model that just doesn't deliver the profit margin needed to keep the doors open. The aspiring herbal entrepreneur wants to keep their products affordable, but if they haven't properly calculated the true cost of production, how can they correctly determine a profitable price point?

The first step to an accurate understanding of the cost of production is properly calculating the true cost of your ingredients, containers, and labels. Every ingredient, no matter how minuscule, needs to be included in your calculations. If you're buying bottles by the case, you'll need to determine the cost per item. If you are purchasing ingredients by the pound, you'll need to calculate the price per ounce. This is the only way to accurately assess your material expense per unit of final product. Be sure to include individual label costs, caps, seals, and anything else that goes into the production of your product.

The next cost to calculate is your time. This is an input that all too often is not included in the final price of the products, especially with new businesses. It's common for a budding new herbalist to assume that not calculating their time is acceptable because they're "doing what they love" or they're concerned that their final price to the consumer will be too high to be competitive in the market—but this is a fallacy! Neglecting this important expense will almost surely negatively impact the longevity of the business. How can the herbalist prosper if they are not being properly compensated for their time?

Once the true, total expense of each product has been determined, the general rule of thumb is to then set the retail price of the item at three times the cost of production. For example: Let's imagine that the artisan herbalist is making one dozen salves for sale at a local craft market. They have determined that the total cost of ingredients, packaging, and labels for that production run is $12. Further, they have decided that they will be paying a labor cost to themselves of $10 per hour, and the total production time for this run was one hour. The total cost to the herbalist for this dozen salves can be calculated at $22, or $1.84 per salve, if we round up. (Always round up.) By using the general rule of three times cost, the herbalist can determine that it would be profitable to sell their salves for $5.52 each. Since we always round up, the retail price of the herbal salve could be set at $6. Of course, this is a simplified example, and it would be up to the herbalist to determine the actual costs of materials and labor for the products they choose to craft and offer commercially.

As the herbal business grows, so will the expenses one must consider for their pricing model, possibly including a website, advertising, booth rentals, or maybe even the cost of a brick-and-mortar location. It's important to stay flexible with your pricing, but remember that it's easier to lower your prices later than it is to raise them.

SELLING AND MARKETING

Once a profitable price point is established, the business owner now needs to decide how and where they will sell their herbal products to the public. There are a number of options here, all of which have their pros and cons. Many new herbal businesses get their start by first offering their goods to family and friends who happily provide the feedback that allows the business owner to tweak and fine-tune their products before offering them to the public. When you are ready to take this step, one of the best places to introduce your line to

Cost vs. Retail Price

(12) 1oz SALVES

Packaging	$3.00
Seals	$0.60
Printing/Labels	$1.50
Beeswax	$2.15
Oil	$3.25
Herb	$1.50
Labor	$10.00

TOTAL COST (12) SALVES $22.00 / 12 =

COST PER 1oz SALVE $1.84

GENERAL RULE OF THUMB
COST x 3 = RETAIL PRICE

$1.84 x 3 = $5.52

Always round up!

**RETAIL PRICE
$6 or above**

▲ Calculating the costs of manufacturing products can help the artisan herbalist properly determine a profitable price point.

potential customers is through a local farmers market or craft show. These are usually inexpensive opportunities that don't require more than a one-day commitment, and they allow the herbalist a chance to chat with customers, further define their brand, and begin to build awareness about the work they are doing. This can be a lot of fun. There will be opportunities to set up and decorate the table, share knowledge with interested shoppers, and even to meet other vendors and learn from their experiences. Once you find a market that responds well to your presence, try to stick with it for a season; building a customer base and having "regulars" can really help get your business up and on its feet. Some days will be frustrating. There may be low traffic or bad weather, but perseverance is the key to success.

Another important avenue to investigate for marketing and direct sales to customers is the internet. One of the greatest benefits of online sales platforms is the potentially limitless reach that the internet affords you in contrast to the finite number of customers that can be reached at a market or other tabled event. If you decide that online sales are an option you'd like to pursue, the next decision is whether to list your products on a third-party platform or if you're ready to launch your own personal business website. Early in your business's life, a combination of both options may be the best course of action. While a third-party sales site, such as Etsy, already draws daily customers in the thousands, the site may have dozens of other companies somewhat similar to yours vying for the same attention. However, getting a storefront set up on one these sites is relatively inexpensive, and you are typically only charged a small percentage of your sales each month. Launching a dedicated website for your business may involve a significantly larger investment, but, as you develop and establish your brand, you may quickly realize the value of these upfront costs. A templated website program such as Wix or WordPress will certainly make this process a bit less complicated, especially for the business owner unable to afford hiring a webmaster to build and manage a site. Regardless of the online platform you choose, you'll need some high-quality images of your products to properly showcase them. Consider trying to take these initial photos yourself, as hiring a photographer for product shots can quickly become too expensive to support your pricing model.

Another potential direction that the herbalist might take is selling their products wholesale to retailers. This can be a great avenue to increase exposure by getting your brand into stores and in front of a demographic of shoppers that might be interested in your product. Typically, retailers will want to purchase your products by the case at 40% to 55% of the retail price.

If you have friends or colleagues that own a co-op or health food store in your area, selling with them first may prove to be a good way to introduce yourself to the wholesale market while allowing you the opportunity to work through the details of pricing and order fulfillment before heading out to shop your brand to the larger retailers that might be a good fit for your business.

Some businesses work exclusively through the wholesale market, while others prefer the direct sales route, and yet others enjoy a hybrid business model that incorporates a number of sales channels to reach the consumer. It is up to you to decide which model you prefer and what best fits your goals as a business owner—as well as your resources and available time. However, if you are planning to potentially delve into the world of wholesale business, be sure that your pricing model allows you to match the retailers' needs while still allowing you a profit margin comfortable enough for your business to remain viable.

ADVERTISING

Now that you have your product line, pricing, and sales channels set up, it's time to get the word out about your awesome new herbal business! A traditional advertising campaign would include such standards as business cards, logoed merchandise, radio spots, and print ads in the local press. While these may still be valuable parts of an advertising campaign, the costs involved can quickly add up, and it can prove difficult to measure your return on investment. Business cards, however, are always recommended, not only for dispersing at events or with purchases, but also so you can have them handy to give out at those chance meetings with potential clients, wholesale account reps, or other like-minded herbal friends.

It's highly recommended that the aspiring herbal business owner look to social media platforms, as these are the easiest and least expensive way to build brand awareness, interact with current and potential customers, and drive sales traffic to a website or event. There are, of course, many social media websites, and each targets a different consumer demographic; the herbalist should choose one or a combination of sites depending on the customer base they are seeking and the amount of time they are willing to dedicate to keeping all the sites current and active. Positive results with social media are driven by content and regular interaction. To reap the greatest benefit from these platforms, one must be willing to learn how they best operate and set aside the time needed to take advantage of the sites to their fullest.

Thankfully, many people are already using these sites daily in their personal life, so the transition to a more commercial application can be relatively easy to achieve.

One very useful way to stay in touch with customers and fans of your herbal business is by maintaining a list of email contacts. There are a number of free (or relatively inexpensive) database and email template services available that will help you keep contact information organized and useful. Try to capture people's contact information whenever possible, whether it's through a sign-up sheet on your event table or through a portal on your business website. Maintaining direct contact with people who have expressed an interest in your company is the easiest and most effective way to build a client base and establish return customers—which is one of the most valuable assets for any business.

◀ Capture quality images of your products at home using a tripod, natural lighting, and a plain background.

LAWS AND REGULATIONS

It's always imperative to ensure that your herbal business is operating within the parameters of the law. As a startup, it's all too easy to be tempted to skip this step, hoping to "fly under the radar." Assuming your new business is too small to be noticed is a decision that can quickly come back to haunt you. Understanding the specific regulations in your field and how they relate to your work can seem daunting and overwhelming at first, but the same authorities that enforce these rules are also there to help guide you through the process, and they are usually willing to help you find ways to comply with the necessary legal parameters.

Reach out to your local small business organizations, or even your nearest Chamber of Commerce or Small Business Development Center. These groups should be able to get you started on the path to understanding which regulating bodies dictate the laws for your particular herbal business venture.

Through these organizations, you will learn about any potential licensing, production facility requirements, labeling laws, and tax-related paperwork that may be needed to get your business up and running. Remember, although this may seem confusing or intimidating, these organizations are in place to help you succeed, and they will guide and encourage you through every step of the process and will do their best to help your fledgling business succeed.

SELF-CARE

It is far too easy to glorify *busyness*. After all, as entrepreneurs, we know that overwhelming busyness is usually seen as an indicator of economic success. We want to be busy, to push ourselves to the limit as we strive to achieve our dreams, but we also need to set time aside for our bodies and souls to recharge. Running oneself to exhaustion is simply not sustainable. While pricing, labeling, packaging, licensing, and marketing are all immensely important components of a successful business venture, if, at the end of the day, the entrepreneur doesn't have the time or energy to enjoy the fruits of their labor, then truly what's the point? Joy is the most important ingredient of true success.

As artisan herbalists, it's important that we dedicate a portion of each day to self-care. Whether this is in the form of meditation, yoga, exercise, or a walk in the park is up to the individual, but it is crucial that this time be considered just as valuable as time spent creating recipes and products or selling and marketing to customers. If you forget to care for yourself and don't set time aside to recharge, every aspect of your business will suffer. Remember, you are your business's greatest asset.

ABOUT THE AUTHOR

BEVIN COHEN is an author, herbalist, gardener, seed saver, and educator. He is the owner of Small House Farm, a sustainable herb farm in central Michigan, offering a full line of herbal wellness products crafted from herbs that are grown or gathered from the wild and oils that are cold-pressed at the homestead. The products are sold across the US and have been featured in numerous magazines. Cohen offers workshops and lectures nationwide on the benefits of living closer to the land through seeds, herbs, and locally grown food. He is the author of *From Our Seeds & Their Keepers* and *Saving Our Seeds*. He serves on the boards of the International Herb Association, the Slow Food Ark of Taste Seed Bank, and the advisory council for the Community Seed Network. He lives in Sanford, Michigan.

A NOTE ABOUT THE PUBLISHER

New Society Publishers is an activist, solutions-oriented publisher focused on publishing books for a world of change. Our books offer tips, tools, and insights from leading experts in sustainable building, homesteading, climate change, environment, conscientious commerce, renewable energy, and more—positive solutions for troubled times.

We're proud to hold to the highest environmental and social standards of any publisher in North America. When you buy New Society books, you are part of the solution!

- We print all our books in North America, never overseas
- All our books are printed on 100% post-consumer recycled paper, processed chlorine free, with low-VOC vegetable-based inks (since 2002)
- Our corporate structure is an innovative employee shareholder agreement, so we're one-third employee-owned (since 2015)
- We're carbon-neutral (since 2006)
- We're certified as a B Corporation (since 2016)

At New Society Publishers, we care deeply about what we publish–but also about how we do business.

MIX
Paper from responsible sources
FSC® C016245

new society
PUBLISHERS
www.newsociety.com

ENVIRONMENTAL BENEFITS STATEMENT

New Society Publishers saved the following resources by printing the pages of this book on chlorine free paper made with 100% post-consumer waste.

TREES	WATER	ENERGY	SOLID WASTE	GREENHOUSE GASES
39	**3,100**	**16**	**140**	**16,800**
FULLY GROWN	GALLONS	MILLION BTUs	POUNDS	POUNDS

Environmental impact estimates were made using the Environmental Paper Network Paper Calculator 4.0. For more information visit www.papercalculator.org.